GCSE English Literature AQA Anthology

The Study Guide

Poems from
Duffy, Armitage, pre-1914

AQA A Specification — Foundation Level

This book is a step-by-step guide to becoming an expert on the Anthology part of your GCSE English Literature exam.

It's got everything you need to know — annotated poems, exam themes and worked essays.

It's ideal for use as a classroom study book or a revision guide.

What CGP is all about

Our sole aim here at CGP is to produce the highest quality books — carefully written, immaculately presented and dangerously close to being funny.

Then we work our socks off to get them out to you — at the cheapest possible prices.

CONTENTS

CGP

A change to Carol Ann Duffy poems

As you might have heard, the AQA exam board have decided to remove *Education for Leisure* by Carol Ann Duffy from their Anthology.

If you're doing your exam in 2009 it won't be in any questions, but you can still refer to it in your answers if you like.

If you're doing your exam in 2010, the poem will have gone altogether — so there's no need to study it at all. For 2010, *Elvis's Twin Sister* by Carol Ann Duffy will be a Key Poem instead.

ZAFP41

Section Three — Simon Armitage

Section Four — Themes: Ideas, Attitudes and Feelings

Section Five — Themes: Methods of Poetry

Section Six — How to Answer the Question

☆ = Key poems as suggested by AQA

Published by Coordination Group Publications Ltd.

Editors:

Charley Darbishire, Kate Houghton, Kate Redmond, Katherine Reed, Edward Robinson.

Contributors:

Margaret Giordmaine, Roland Haynes, Shelagh Moore, Elisabeth Sanderson, Nicola Woodfin.

With thanks to Kate Houghton and Barbara Brecht for the proofreading.

ISBN: 978 1 84146 814 3

Groovy website: www.cgpbooks.co.uk

Jolly bits of clipart from CorelDRAW®
Printed by Elanders Hindson Ltd, Newcastle upon Tyne.

How To Use This Book

This book will help you to do better in your GCSE English Literature Anthology Exam. It's full of straightforward ways of getting extra marks. Start by asking your teacher which poems and themes you need to study: some schools get you to study all of them, others pick out certain ones.

There are Six Sections in this book

Sections One, Two and Three are about the Poems

There are two pages about each poem. This is what the pages look like:

There's a nice picture of the poet and some info about their life.

Important or tricky bits of the poem are highlighted and explained.

Difficult words are defined in the poem dictionary.

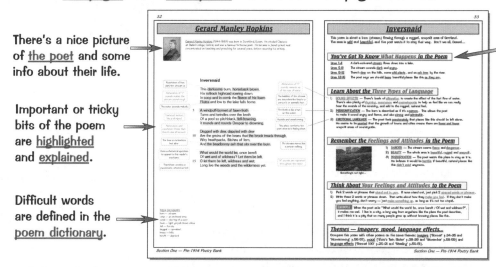

On the right-hand page there are notes about the poem. They include:

• what happens in the poem.

• the language the poet uses.

• the feelings of the poet.

• a bit that'll help you write about your personal response to the poem.

Read through the pages on the poems you've been told to study. When you've read about each poem, shut the book and write out as much as you can remember. See what you've left out, then do it again.

Sections Four and Five are about the Themes

In the exam, you'll have to compare how four poems relate to one of the themes. In Sections Four and Five, there's a page about each of the main themes that might come up. The pages tell you which poems use each theme and how different poets treat the same theme. Read them, understand them and learn them.

Section Six is about Preparing for your Exam

Pages 84-85 tell you how to plan and write good essays using CGP's 6-step method. The section also includes exam questions with sample answers. This is what they look like:

Sample exam question.

A sample plan for how you could answer the exam question.

A sample student answer, which continues on the opposite page.

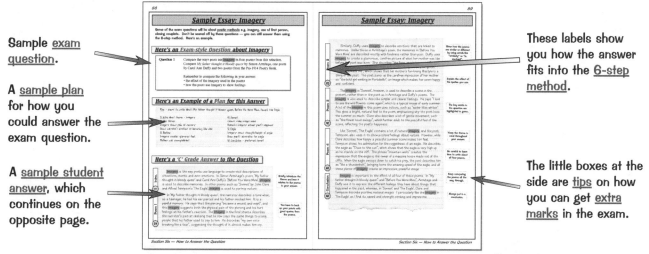

These labels show you how the answer fits into the 6-step method.

The little boxes at the side are tips on how you can get extra marks in the exam.

Write some essays using the 6-step method. Use the exam-style questions in CGP's foundation level Duffy and Armitage Anthology Workbook, if you have it, or ask your teacher for some practice questions. You get one hour to answer the question in the exam, so practise doing some timed essays.

Ben Jonson

Key Poem

Ben Jonson (1572-1637) was the son of a clergyman. He attended Westminster School, before becoming a bricklayer and later joining the army. He went on to become one of the most important poets of his time. He also wrote plays and was a friend of William Shakespeare.

The poem is written directly to his son. It's his way of saying a fond goodbye.

On my first Sonne

He loved his son very much.

His "sinne" was hoping that his son would live for a long time.

Farewell, thou child of my right hand, and joy;
My sinne was too much hope of thee, lov'd boy,
Seven yeeres tho'wert lent to me, and I thee pay,
Exacted by thy fate, on the just day.
5 O, could I loose all father, now. For why
Will man lament the state he should envie?
To have so soone scap'd worlds, and fleshes rage,
And, if no other miserie, yet age?
Rest in soft peace, and, ask'd, say here doth lye
10 Ben. Jonson his best piece of poetrie.
For whose sake, hence-forth, all his vowes be such,
As what he loves may never like too much.

Uses money as a metaphor. Jonson's son was "lent" to him for seven years and now he has to "pay" his debt through the death of his son.

Shows his affection for his son.

Says there are advantages to being dead, e.g. you don't have to suffer pain and old age.

His son was his greatest creation.

This type of language is usually found on a gravestone — the poem is a tribute to Jonson's son.

He decides he'll never love anyone else so much because he doesn't want to feel so much pain again.

POEM DICTIONARY
sinne — an old way of spelling sin
yeeres — years
tho'wert — you were
lament — to feel sorrow or regret
scap'd — a shortened way of writing escaped
miserie — an old way of spelling misery
hence-forth — from now on

On my first Sonne

This is a simple poem about a father who is <u>mourning</u> the death of his seven year-old <u>son</u>.
The poem is the father's way of <u>saying goodbye</u> to his son.

You've Got to Know What Happens in the Poem

<u>Lines 1-4</u>   The man says <u>goodbye</u> to his seven year old son who has just <u>died</u>.

<u>Lines 5-8</u>   He says he <u>envies</u> his son because in <u>heaven</u> you don't have to
deal with all the <u>horrible</u> things that happen in life.

<u>Lines 9-12</u>   Ben Jonson says that his <u>son</u> was his best ever <u>creation</u>. He decides that in the future he
won't <u>love</u> anyone as much as he loved his son so that he won't get so <u>upset</u> if they die.

Learn About the Three Types of Language

1) <u>PRIDE and AFFECTION</u> — The poet is very <u>fond</u> of his son. The poem is written as though he's
<u>talking directly</u> to him. This makes it seem very <u>personal</u> and helps you to imagine the poet's <u>feelings</u>.

2) <u>METAPHORICAL LANGUAGE</u> — The poet uses a metaphor about <u>debt</u> and <u>money</u>
to describe the loss of his son.

3) <u>COMMENTS ABOUT DEATH</u> — There are quite a few different ideas about <u>death</u> in this poem.
On one hand the poet is <u>sad</u> that his son's dead, on the other he says that early death isn't
all bad because you don't have to <u>grow old</u> and suffer <u>pain</u>.

Remember the Feelings and Attitudes in the Poem

Rest in
Soft Peace

1) <u>GRIEF</u> — The poet is really <u>upset</u> about the <u>death</u> of his son.

2) <u>UNCERTAINTY</u> — The poet <u>wonders</u> whether it is better
to be dead than to be alive.

3) <u>PAIN</u> — He's so <u>devastated</u> by his son's death that he decides never to love
anyone else as much, because he doesn't want to <u>suffer</u> like this again.

Think About Your Feelings and Attitudes to the Poem

1) Pick 2 words or phrases that <u>stand out to you</u>. If none stand out, just pick 2 unusual words or phrases.

2) Write these 2 words or phrases down. Then write about how they <u>make you feel</u>. If they don't make you
feel anything, don't worry — just <u>make something up</u>, as long as it's <u>not too stupid</u>.

> EXAMPLE   I find it very touching that the poet describes his son as his
> "best piece of poetrie". Even though he was such a good poet, he thinks
> that having a son was a greater achievement than his writing.

Themes — death, parent/child relationships, love...

You can compare this poem with other poems about the same themes: <u>death</u> ('Tichborne's Elegy'
p.14-15), <u>parent/child relationships</u> ('Before You Were Mine' p.44-45, 'Mother, any distance'
p.52-53 and 'Kid' p.60-61), and <u>love</u> ('Anne Hathaway' p.40-41).

William Butler Yeats

<u>William Butler Yeats</u> (1865-1939) was born in Dublin. He is often considered to be Ireland's greatest ever poet. As well as poetry, Yeats wrote many plays and won the Nobel Prize for Literature. He was also involved in the Celtic Revival, a movement to encourage traditional Irish culture and discourage English influences on Ireland.

Shows the poem is from the point of view of the old mother.

The old woman gets up really early whilst the young people lie about in bed.

Young people only care about unimportant things.

The woman thinks that young people are always moaning.

The woman has no choice but to work.

The poem is in rhyming couplets.

List of all the rubbish jobs that the old woman has to do.

Slow, plodding rhythm suggests the boring, repetitive tasks.

The Song of the Old Mother

I rise in the dawn, and I kneel and blow
Till the seed of the fire flicker and glow;
And then I must scrub and bake and sweep
Till stars are beginning to blink and peep;
5 And the young lie long and dream in their bed
Of the matching of ribbons for bosom and head,
And their day goes over in idleness,
And they sigh if the wind but lift a tress:
While I must work because I am old,
10 And the seed of the fire gets feeble and cold.

The woman gets the fire going in the morning, but by the end of the day it's going out — she'll have to do it all again the next day.

The woman's work makes her tired and weak, just as the fire gets weaker as the day goes on.

<u>POEM DICTIONARY</u>
tress — a lock of hair

The Song of the Old Mother

In this poem an <u>old woman</u> describes the daily <u>chores</u> she has to do. She seems to think that people in younger generations are a bit lazy and that they have a much easier life than she does.

You've Got to Know What Happens in the Poem

<u>Lines 1-2</u>	The old woman gets up and gets the <u>fire</u> going.
<u>Lines 3-4</u>	She does <u>cooking</u> and <u>cleaning</u> until night time.
<u>Lines 5-8</u>	The woman thinks that <u>younger people</u> (possibly her children) are <u>lazy</u> and that they don't have to do as much <u>hard work</u> as she has to.
<u>Line 9-10</u>	The woman sums up her <u>attitude</u> to <u>life</u>, and the <u>fire</u> she has made starts to <u>go out</u>.

Learn About the Two Types of Language

1) <u>RHYMING COUPLETS AND RHYTHM</u> — the <u>rhyming couplets</u> make the poem sound <u>repetitive</u> like the woman's <u>work</u>. The <u>regular rhythm</u> also makes the poem read like a <u>song</u> which ties in with the <u>title</u> of the poem.

2) <u>CONTRAST</u> — Yeats points out all the <u>differences</u> between the life that the old woman lives and the spoilt lives of the young people.

Remember the Feelings and Attitudes in the Poem

1) <u>SYMPATHY</u> — The poet <u>feels sorry</u> for the old mother.

2) <u>HARD WORK</u> — The poet thinks that the woman's life will <u>inevitably</u> carry on like this until she <u>dies</u>.

3) <u>MORALS</u> — Yeats uses the poem to show people what life is like for <u>old people</u> who have to do lots of <u>work</u> — perhaps he hopes that it will <u>change</u> people's attitudes towards poor elderly people.

Think About Your Feelings and Attitudes to the Poem

1) Pick 2 words or phrases that <u>stand out to you</u>. If none stand out, just pick 2 unusual words or phrases.

2) Write these 2 words or phrases down. Then write about how they <u>make you feel</u>. If they don't make you feel anything, don't worry — just <u>make something up</u>, as long as it's <u>not too stupid</u>.

> **EXAMPLE** The phrase "lie long and dream in their bed" makes me feel sympathy for the woman in the poem and anger towards the lazy young people. The phrase highlights the difference between the lives of the young people and the old woman's life.

Themes — attitudes to others, first person, imagery...

You could compare this poem with other poems about the same themes: <u>attitudes towards other people</u> ('Before You Were Mine' p.44-45 and 'November' p.58-59), <u>use of first person</u> ('The Affliction of Margaret' p.10-11) and <u>imagery</u> ('Homecoming' p.56-57).

William Wordsworth

Talks to him directly again.

My Son, if thou be humbled, poor,
Hopeless of honour and of gain,
Oh! do not dread thy mother's door;
Think not of me with grief and pain:
40 I now can see with better eyes;
And worldly grandeur I despise,
And fortune with her gifts and lies.

Nothing but her son matters to her now.

She thinks that birds have fate on their side — but she doesn't.

Alas! the fowls of Heaven have wings,
And blasts of Heaven will aid their flight;
45 They mount – how short a voyage brings
The Wanderers back to their delight!
Chains tie us down by land and sea;
And wishes, vain as mine, may be
All that is left to comfort thee.

50 Perhaps some dungeon hears thee groan,
Maimed, mangled by inhuman men;
Or thou upon a Desart thrown
Inheritest the Lion's Den;
Or hast been summon'd to the Deep,
55 Thou, Thou, and all thy mates, to keep
An incommunicable sleep.

Words of pain and torture — she can only imagine the worst in this verse.

A desperate and irrational way of trying to deal with her situation.

I look for Ghosts; but none will force
Their way to me; 'tis falsely said
That there was ever intercourse
60 Betwixt the living and the dead;
For, surely, then I should have sight
Of Him I wait for day and night,
With love and longings infinite.

Her greatest fear is not being able to talk to him.

She seems to worship him.

My apprehensions come in crowds;
65 I dread the rustling of the grass;
The very shadows of the clouds
Have power to shake me as they pass;
I question things, and do not find
One that will answer to my mind;
70 And all the world appears unkind.

Her worries come to her randomly — she can't control her thoughts.

She can't be happy about anything.

Her worries have made her weak.

Beyond participation lie
My troubles, and beyond relief:
If any chance to heave a sigh
They pity me, and not my grief.
75 Then come to me, my Son, or send
Some tidings that my woes may end;
I have no other earthly friend.

She feels that no one could understand how strong her grief is.

POEM DICTIONARY
affliction — pain
prosperous — rich
undone — ruined
beguiled — fooled
ingenuous — open, honest
ensued — followed
base — bad, corrupt
incommunicable —
        too far away to talk with
intercourse — conversation
betwixt — between
infinite — never-ending
apprehensions — fears
tidings — news

William Wordsworth

William Wordsworth (1770-1850) was one of England's greatest poets.
He was born in Cockermouth, and wrote many poems about the Lake District.
He went to Cambridge University. He was made Poet Laureate in 1843.

The Affliction of Margaret

Margaret addresses her son directly in the first stanza.

She's looking for answers, trying to make sense of her son's disappearance.

Where art thou, my beloved Son,
Where art thou, worse to me than dead?
Oh find me, prosperous or undone!
Or, if the grave be now thy bed,
5   Why am I ignorant of the same
That I may rest; and neither blame,
Nor sorrow may attend thy name?

She's desperate to find him, whether he's rich, poor or dead.

Seven years, alas! to have received
No tidings of an only child;
10   To have despaired, and have believed,
And be for evermore beguiled;
Sometimes with thoughts of very bliss!
I catch at them, and then I miss;
Was ever darkness like to this?

Her pain seems to last for ever.

Her lack of knowledge.

15   He was among the prime in worth,
An object beauteous to behold;
Well born, well bred; I sent him forth
Ingenuous, innocent, and bold:
If things ensued that wanted grace,
20   As hath been said, they were not base;
And never blush was on my face.

She remembers only the best things about him.

She won't accept any criticism of him.

Ah! little doth the Young One dream,
When full of play and childish cares,
What power hath even his wildest scream,
25   Heard by his Mother unawares!
He knows it not, he cannot guess:
Years to a Mother bring distress;
But do not make her love the less.

This fits in with the idea of innocence in the previous verse.

She's struggling to control her emotions.

Neglect me! no I suffered long
30   From that ill thought; and being blind,
Said, 'Pride shall help me in my wrong;
Kind mother have I been, as kind
As ever breathed:' and that is true;
I've wet my path with tears like dew,
35   Weeping for him when no one knew.

She's blind to the truth.

Simile creates an image of gentle but constant crying.

She's suffered on her own.

THIS IS A FLAP.
FOLD THIS PAGE OUT.

The Affliction of Margaret

The poet describes the feelings of Margaret, a woman whose <u>son</u> has been <u>missing</u> for seven years. She <u>fears the worst</u>, and she's desperate to talk to him.

You've Got to Know What Happens in the Poem

<u>Lines 1-14</u>	Margaret describes the <u>pain</u> of not knowing <u>where her son is</u>.
<u>Lines 15-21</u>	She goes on about how <u>good-looking</u> and <u>well-meaning</u> her son was.
<u>Lines 22-28</u>	She says children <u>don't realise</u> how much their <u>mothers worry</u> about them.
<u>Lines 29-42</u>	Margaret says she was a <u>good mother</u>. She wants her son to <u>return</u>, whatever state he's in.
<u>Lines 43-49</u>	She says that <u>birds</u> have wings, so they're <u>free</u> to return. People <u>don't have</u> this freedom.
<u>Lines 50-56</u>	She imagines terrible things happening to her son, like being <u>imprisoned</u> or <u>shipwrecked</u>.
<u>Lines 57-70</u>	She says it's <u>impossible</u> to talk to the <u>dead</u>. There's <u>no escape</u> from her fears.
<u>Lines 71-77</u>	<u>No-one</u> can understand her grief. Her son <u>returning</u> to her is the only way to end it.

Learn About the Three Types of Language

1) <u>OBSESSIVE LANGUAGE</u> — Thoughts of Margaret's son have completely <u>taken over</u> her life. Her thoughts are <u>illogical</u>, and she feels she <u>can't be happy</u> about anything while her son's still missing.

2) <u>PAIN and FEAR</u> — She seems to <u>torture herself</u> by thinking of all the <u>awful things</u> that might have happened to him. She feels that it would be better to know he was dead than not to know anything.

3) <u>REFLECTIVE LANGUAGE</u> — She's sometimes more <u>reasoning</u>, trying to find answers. She feels she <u>can't explain</u> her feelings to anyone — she's <u>alone</u> with her sorrow, and desperate just to <u>talk</u> to her son.

Remember the Feelings and Attitudes in the Poem

"I hope he's got some clean underpants..."

1) <u>SYMPATHY</u> — The poet <u>feels sorry</u> for Margaret.
2) <u>ANXIETY</u> — He shows how <u>anxious</u> she is to find out how her son is.
3) <u>DESPERATION</u> — She feels absolutely <u>desperate</u> — nothing matters to her but her son.

Margaret's quite <u>irrational</u> at times — she tries to talk to her son even though he's not there, and her mind jumps from one thought to another fairly randomly.

Think About Your Feelings and Attitudes to the Poem

1) Pick 2 words or phrases that <u>stand out to you</u>. If none stand out, just pick 2 <u>unusual words or phrases</u>.

2) Write these 2 words or phrases down. Then write about how they <u>make you feel</u>. If they don't make you feel anything, don't worry — just <u>make something up</u>, as long as it's not too stupid.

> EXAMPLE The phrase "I've wet my path with tears like dew" makes me feel really sorry for Margaret. It seems there is no end to her suffering, and her pain follows her wherever she goes.

Themes — parent/child relationships, strong emotions...

You could compare 'The Affliction of Margaret' with other poems about the same themes: <u>parent/child relationships</u> ('On my first Sonne' p.6-7 and 'Mother, any distance' p.52-53) and <u>strong emotions</u> ('Havisham' p.36-37 and 'Kid' p.60-61).

William Blake

<u>William Blake</u> (1757-1827) was born in London and educated at home by his mother. He was a poet, artist, engraver and publisher. He believed in the power of the imagination and religion over material things.

The Little Boy Lost

The boy calls after his dad, but "father" could also mean God.

'Father, father, where are you going?
Oh do not walk so fast!
Speak, father, speak to your little boy
Or else I shall be lost.'

The boy sounds desperate and helpless.

5   The night was dark, no father was there,
The child was wet with dew;
The mire was deep, and the child did weep,
And away the vapour flew.

The child seems doomed on his own.

The Little Boy Found

This can be interpreted in different ways. The light could be like the star that led the wise men to the baby Jesus. Or it could be a bad spirit that is leading the little boy into danger.

The little boy lost in the lonely fen,
Led by the wand'ring light,
Began to cry; but God, ever nigh,
Appeared like his father in white.

Suggests God is always there for you when you need him.

God is a much better father to the boy than his actual father.

5   He kissed the child, and by the hand led,
And to his mother brought,
Who in sorrow pale, through the lonely dale
Her little boy weeping sought.

The boy's mum seems devoted and loving — unlike his dad who failed to look after him.

God shows the boy the way home — compare this with line 5 above.

The mother has been crying, just like the boy.

<u>POEM DICTIONARY</u>
mire — mud
vapour — mist
fen — a marshy area
nigh — near
dale — a valley in a hilly area

The Little Boy Lost and The Little Boy Found

These two poems go together to tell a sweet little tale about a little boy who gets lost...
and then gets found again, with a bit of help from God. The poems have a <u>religious message</u>
— the poet says that God will show us the way when we're lost.

You've Got to Know What Happens in the Poems

<u>The Little Boy Lost</u>

<u>Lines 1-4</u>   A little boy calls out to his <u>dad</u>, asking him to wait so he doesn't get <u>lost</u>.

<u>Lines 5-8</u>   But his dad disappears, leaving the boy <u>lost</u> and <u>crying</u>.

<u>The Little Boy Found</u>

<u>Lines 1-4</u>   The boy's <u>lost</u> on his own, but luckily for him, <u>God</u> shows up.

<u>Lines 5-8</u>   God leads the boy back to his <u>mum</u>, who was out <u>looking for him</u>.

Learn About the Two Types of Language

1)   <u>EMOTIVE LANGUAGE</u> — The poet's descriptions of the boy make him seem <u>helpless</u> and <u>vulnerable</u>.
This makes the reader <u>pity him</u>. It also shows how he <u>can't cope</u> on his own.

2)   <u>RELIGIOUS LANGUAGE</u> — There's lots of <u>Christian imagery</u> in the poem. This supports the overall
<u>religious message</u> — that we are <u>lost without God</u>, and can only find safety with his help.

Remember the Feelings and Attitudes in the Poems

These two poems are a bit boring, so here's
a picture of something more exciting.

1)   <u>FEAR</u> — The boy is <u>desperate</u> and <u>scared</u>.

2)   <u>CONCERN</u> — His mother is <u>worried sick</u> about her son.

3)   <u>RELIGION</u> — The poet believes people are only <u>safe</u> when
they're with <u>God</u>. He thinks people are <u>lost without God</u>.

Think About Your Feelings and Attitudes to the Poems

1)   Pick 2 words or phrases that <u>stand out to you</u>. If none stand out, just pick 2 <u>unusual words or phrases</u>.

2)   Write these 2 words or phrases down. Then write about how they <u>make you feel</u>. If they don't make
you feel anything, don't worry — just <u>make something up</u>, as long as it's not too stupid.

> **EXAMPLE**   When the child says "Speak, father, speak to your little boy", I feel really
> sorry for him. He seems completely helpless and unable to survive on his own.

Themes — danger, strong emotions, imagery...

Compare this poem with other poems on the same themes: <u>danger</u> ('Stealing' p.50-51 and 'Hitcher'
p.66-67), <u>strong emotions</u> ('The Affliction of Margaret' p.10-11 and 'My father thought it bloody
queer' p.54-55) and <u>imagery</u> ('Havisham' p.36-37 and 'Mother, any distance' p.52-53).

Chidiock Tichborne

<u>Chidiock Tichborne</u> (c.1558-1586) was a Roman Catholic. He was part of a plot to murder Elizabeth I and replace her with the Catholic Mary Queen of Scots. The plot was discovered and Chidiock was arrested and condemned to death. He wrote this poem in a letter to his wife, Agnes, just before his death. He was hung, drawn and quartered in 1586, at the age of 28.

Tichborne's Elegy

Written with his own hand in the Tower before his execution

This is supposed to be the best bit of his life.

All these lines are phrased in the same way.

My prime of youth is but a frost of cares,
My feast of joy is but a dish of pain;
My crop of corn is but a field of tares,
And all my good is but vain hope of gain.
5 The day is past, and yet I saw no sun;
And now I live, and now my life is done.

Gloomy language.

The day represents life, the sun represents enjoyment of life.

This line is repeated at the end of the other two verses as well.

The fallen fruit represents his death, the green leaves represent his youth.

My tale was heard, and yet it was not told,
My fruit is fallen, and yet my leaves are green;
My youth is spent, and yet I am not old,
10 I saw the world, and yet I was not seen.
My thread is cut, and yet it is not spun;
And now I live, and now my life is done.

The repetition of "and yet" emphasises the irony of his situation — his life's over, and yet he's still young.

The lines in this verse sound like riddles.

Nearly every word in the poem has just one syllable, making it sound plain and direct.

I sought my death, and found it in my womb,
I looked for life and saw it was a shade;
15 I trod the earth, and knew it was my tomb,
And now I die, and now I was but made.
My glass is full, and now my glass is run;
And now I live, and now my life is done.

Contrast: end of life and beginning of life.

He's convinced he's going to die.

The poem has a regular rhyme scheme.

He hasn't got any hope.

POEM DICTIONARY
elegy — a song or verse commemorating a dead person
tares — weeds
shade — old-fashioned word for a ghost

Tichborne's Elegy

Chidiock Tichborne was about to be <u>executed</u> when he wrote this poem. Unsurprisingly, he's not too chuffed about the idea of <u>dying</u>. Little did he know that he would find everlasting life in the pages of the GCSE AQA English Literature Anthology...

You've Got to Know *What Happens* in the Poem

<u>Lines 1-6</u>   Tichborne contrasts his <u>health and youth</u> with the fact that he's about to <u>die</u>.
                    He uses a series of <u>metaphors</u> to represent his situation.

<u>Lines 7-12</u>   Another verse on the <u>same theme</u>, also using metaphors.

<u>Lines 13-18</u>   This verse is similar to the other two, but this one mentions <u>death</u> directly.
                    All three verses <u>end with the same line</u>, which sums up his fate:
                    "And now I live, and now my life is done."

Learn About the *Three Types of Language*

1) <u>METAPHORICAL LANGUAGE</u> — Tichborne uses a series of <u>metaphors</u> throughout the poem to make the point that he's really young and healthy, and yet his life's over anyway.

2) <u>REPETITIVE LANGUAGE</u> — The poem has quite a <u>repetitive structure</u>, e.g. each verse ends with the same line. This emphasises his main point — that he's still young, but is about to die.

3) <u>LANGUAGE ABOUT DEATH</u> — Death is the main theme of the poem.
There's lots of <u>miserable language</u> and imagery about death.

Remember the *Feelings and Attitudes* in the Poem

1) <u>INJUSTICE</u> — He thinks it's <u>unfair</u> that he should have to die so young — he's being cut off in his prime.

2) <u>REGRET</u> — He feels <u>sad</u> that's he's got to leave life so soon.

3) <u>BITTERNESS</u> — There's a tiny bit of <u>bitterness</u> about his situation.

4) <u>IRONY</u> — It seems <u>ironic</u> to Tichborne that he's about to die even though he's young and he feels healthy.

Think About *Your Feelings and Attitudes* to the Poem

1) Pick 2 words or phrases that <u>stand out to you</u>. If none stand out, just pick 2 <u>unusual words or phrases</u>.

2) Write these 2 words or phrases down. Then write about how they <u>make you feel</u>. If they don't make you feel anything, don't worry — just <u>make something up</u>, as long as it's not too stupid.

> **EXAMPLE**   I find the line "And now I live, and now my life is done" very moving.
> The poet knows how hopeless his situation is. Many people in that situation might be
> desperately hoping for escape and freedom, but Tichborne faces his fate. I think this is brave.

Themes — *death, irony and mood...*

You could compare 'Tichborne's Elegy' with other poems on the same theme: <u>death</u> ('November' p.58-59 and 'Hitcher' p.66-67), <u>irony</u> ('The Man He Killed' p.16-17 and 'Salome' p.42-43) and <u>mood</u> ('Sonnet' p.34-35 and 'I've made out a will' p.64-65).

Thomas Hardy

Thomas Hardy (1840-1928) was born in Dorset. He trained as an architect before becoming a very well-known novelist. He wrote classic and often controversial books like 'Jude the Obscure' and 'Far from the Madding Crowd', as well as writing poetry.

The Man He Killed

> The whole poem's in speech marks — to make you imagine someone speaking out loud.

'Had he and I but met
By some old ancient inn,
We should have sat us down to wet
Right many a nipperkin!

> The 1st and 3rd lines, and 2nd and 4th lines rhyme all the way through.

> Informal, friendly language — contrasts with the description of the battle in the second verse.

5   'But ranged as infantry,
And staring face to face,
I shot at him as he at me,
And killed him in his place.

> Very simple, straightforward description of dramatic event.

> Repetition of 'because' shows he's finding it hard to think of a reason why he killed the man.

'I shot him dead because –
10   Because he was my foe,
Just so: my foe of course he was;
That's clear enough; although

> He tries to reassure himself that he was right to kill the man.

> Shortened version of "enlist" (to join the army).

'He thought he'd 'list, perhaps,
Off-hand like – just as I –
15   Was out of work – had sold his traps –
No other reason why.

> Informal language.

> The man he killed was probably a nice bloke who just joined up because he needed a job.

> The soldier imagines that the man he killed was similar to himself.

'Yes; quaint and curious war is!
You shoot a fellow down
You'd treat if met where any bar is,
20   Or help to half-a-crown.'

> This line is worded almost like it's a joke — but there's a lot of bitterness in it.

> Suggests that everyone would do the same thing in a battle situation.

> Sounds more like a friend than an enemy.

POEM DICTIONARY
nipperkin — a small amount of beer or liquor
infantry — foot soldiers
foe — enemy
'list — join the army (short for "enlist")
traps — belongings
quaint — odd
help to — lend
half-a-crown — old British coin

The Man He Killed

Key Poem

In this poem, a <u>soldier</u> tells us about a man he <u>killed in battle</u>. He says that even though the man was on the enemy's side, he was probably just a nice, ordinary bloke. He reckons that if he'd met the man in a pub, instead of the battlefield, they might have been <u>friends</u>.

You've Got to Know What Happens in the Poem

Lines 1-4   The soldier says that he could have been <u>friends</u> with the other man, if they had met in an <u>inn</u>.

Lines 5-8   But they met in <u>battle</u>, and shot at each other. The other man was <u>killed</u>.

Lines 9-12   The <u>only reason</u> he killed the other man was that they were <u>on different sides</u>.

Lines 13-16   He imagines that the man he killed may have been very <u>similar to him</u> — only enlisting in the army because he needed work.

Lines 17-20   He sums up the message of the poem. He says that <u>war is a strange business</u> — you kill people you might have been friends with in different circumstances.

Learn About the Three Types of Language

1) <u>COLLOQUIAL LANGUAGE</u> — This means <u>informal language</u> that sounds like everyday speech. The poem is written as if the soldier is speaking to the reader.

2) <u>MATTER-OF-FACT LANGUAGE</u> — The soldier uses fairly matter-of-fact language to describe killing the man. This down-to-earth language <u>contrasts</u> with the serious message behind the poem, and helps to highlight the soldier's feeling of <u>bitterness</u>.

3) <u>THOUGHTFUL LANGUAGE</u> — The soldier thinks quite deeply about what he has done. He <u>empathises</u> with the man he killed — he can imagine what it was like to be him.

Remember the Feelings and Attitudes in the Poem

Make friends, not war.

1) <u>IRONY</u> — The soldier has a <u>sense of irony</u> about the situation — he's killed a man he might have been friends with in different circumstances.

2) <u>PUZZLEMENT</u> — It <u>troubles</u> the soldier that the man he killed was probably quite like himself.

3) <u>TRAGEDY</u> — The poet's <u>making a point</u> about the <u>tragedy of war</u>.

Think About Your Feelings and Attitudes to the Poem

1) Pick 2 words or phrases that <u>stand out to you</u>. If none stand out, just pick 2 <u>unusual words or phrases</u>.

2) Write these 2 words or phrases down. Then write about how they <u>make you feel</u>. If they don't make you feel anything, don't worry — just <u>make something up</u>, as long as it's not too stupid.

> **EXAMPLE**   The line "Yes; quaint and curious war is!" stands out to me because it's like an emotional outburst. All the way through the poem, the narrator sounds very restrained and matter-of-fact, and then suddenly there is this bitter, sarcastic statement. I can imagine the soldier spitting the words out.

Themes — death, irony and first person...

You can compare 'The Man He Killed' with other poems on the same themes: <u>death</u> ('Salome' p.42-43 and 'Education for Leisure' p.48-49), <u>irony</u> ('Tichborne's Elegy' p.14-15) and <u>use of first person</u> ('Ulysses' p.26-27 and 'Those bastards in their mansions' p.62-63).

Walt Whitman

<u>Walt Whitman</u> (1819-1892) was a poet born in New York. He was one of America's earliest great poets, and was also a teacher and journalist.

Repeated to create a strong first impression of the storm.

An evil sound — dramatic and evil atmosphere.

The poem is one long sentence, with every line ending in "-ing" — this gives a feeling of the storm happening right now, going on and on and on.

Patrolling Barnegat

Onomatopoeia used to describe the noise of the sea.

Alliteration of "s" suggests the sounds of the waves of the ocean.

Sharp and dangerous, like a sword.

The patrollers fear the worst.

The beach protects the land from the storm.

Wild, wild the storm, and the sea high running,
Steady the roar of the gale, with incessant undertone muttering,
Shouts of demoniac laughter fitfully piercing and pealing,
Waves, air, midnight, their savagest trinity lashing,
5 Out in the shadows there milk-white combs careering,
On beachy slush and sand spirts of snow fierce slanting,
Where through the murk the easterly death-wind breasting,
Through cutting swirl and spray watchful and firm advancing,
(That in the distance! is that a wreck? is the red signal flaring?)
10 Slush and sand of the beach tireless till daylight wending,
Steadily, slowly, through hoarse roar never remitting,
Along the midnight edge by those milk-white combs careering,
A group of dim, weird forms, struggling, the night confronting,
That savage trinity warily watching.

Makes the elements sound like an attacking force.

Sounds deep, rough and powerful.

The people in the patrol are hard to see in the confusion and chaos of the storm.

Like sentries on look-out.

Alliteration here sounds like the waves crashing down.

The patrollers face up to the enemy (the storm).

POEM DICTIONARY
Barnegat — a bay in New Jersey, USA
incessant — never-ending
undertone — a hushed sound or voice
demoniac — like the devil
pealing — making a long, loud sound
trinity — three things joined together
combs — the tops of waves
careering — moving quickly
breasting — facing, standing square-on
wending — travelling
remitting — stopping

Patrolling Barnegat

The poet describes a fierce <u>storm</u> blowing at night into a bay in America.
Some people are <u>patrolling</u> the beach, standing up to the wild, cold wind. Brrrrrr....

You've Got to Know What Happens in the Poem

<u>Lines 1-6</u>   A big <u>storm</u> is raging on a beach at night. Strong <u>winds</u> make massive <u>waves</u>
in the sea which batter the land.

<u>Lines 7-14</u>   Amid the dark and bleak night, people <u>patrol</u> the beach, facing up to the storm.
They wonder if they can see a <u>shipwreck</u> in the distance (line 9).

Learn About the Two Types of Language

1) <u>WAR-LIKE LANGUAGE</u> — The storm is like a <u>battleground</u> between land and sea.
The people on patrol on the beach are there to protect the land from attack.

2) <u>SOUNDS OF THE STORM</u> — There's lots of <u>alliteration</u> and <u>onomatopoeia</u>
(words which sound like what they're describing). The poet uses these to
create a sense of the <u>sounds</u> of the howling <u>wind</u> and roaring <u>waves</u>.

Remember the Feelings and Attitudes in the Poem

1) <u>RESPECT</u> — The poet <u>respects</u> the power of the storm.
2) <u>ADMIRATION</u> — He <u>admires</u> the bravery of the
people patrolling the beach.
3) <u>WARINESS</u> — The people patrolling the beach
are <u>cautious</u> (line 14).

There's a sense of <u>dread</u> surrounding the storm
— the storm seems capable of great destruction.

Think About Your Feelings and Attitudes to the Poem

1) Pick 2 words or phrases that <u>stand out to you</u>. If none stand out, just pick 2 <u>unusual words or phrases</u>.

2) Write these 2 words or phrases down. Then write about how they <u>make you feel</u>. If they don't make
you feel anything, don't worry — just <u>make something up</u>, as long as it's not too stupid.

EXAMPLE   The description of the storm as a "savage trinity" fills me with fear. It sounds like
a wild animal, with the three forces of the waves, air and night wildly attacking the land.

Themes — mood, danger and language effects...

Compare 'Patrolling Barnegat' with other poems on the same themes: <u>mood</u> ('We Remember Your
Childhood Well' p.46-47), <u>danger</u> ('Stealing' p.50-51 and 'Those bastards in their mansions'
p.62-63) and <u>language effects</u> ('The Eagle' p.24-25 and 'Inversnaid' p.32-33).

William Shakespeare

William Shakespeare (1564-1616) was a successful playwright and poet. He was born in Stratford-upon-Avon, Warwickshire, but lived in London for most of his life. He is one of the most important literary figures of all time.

Sonnet 130

My mistress' eyes are nothing like the sun;
Coral is far more red than her lips' red.
If snow be white, why then her breasts are dun;
If hairs be wires, black wires grow on her head.
5 I have seen roses damasked, red and white,
But no such roses see I in her cheeks;
And in some perfumes is there more delight
Than in the breath that from my mistress reeks.
I love to hear her speak, yet well I know
10 That music hath a far more pleasing sound.
I grant I never saw a goddess go:
My mistress when she walks treads on the ground.
    And yet, by heaven, I think my love as rare
    As any she belied with false compare.

The word "nothing" changes this line from a compliment into a criticism.

These words might be found in a normal love poem.

Sounds ugly and coarse.

Alternate lines rhyme for the first 12 lines.

Particularly nasty word — makes her sound disgusting.

This woman's real — not some romantic ideal.

The sonnet ends with a rhyming couplet.

These lines start as if they're going to be traditional compliments.

In most love poems, the woman would be compared favourably to these things.

This is the big turning point in the poem. He does love something about her.

He's says he's never seen a goddess, so can't compare her to one.

The last two lines are inset, making them stand out.

Any woman.

This exclamation shows real feeling. He does love her after all.

POEM DICTIONARY
dun — a brownish-grey colour
damasked — damask roses are a type of sweet-smelling rose, damask is a type of embroidered fabric
reeks — stinks
belied — misrepresented, shown to be false

Sonnet 130

Shakespeare spends most of the poem <u>criticising</u> his lover — she's not beautiful, she smells, her hair's all coarse like wire... Then he turns it all around by saying he <u>loves her</u> anyway. You have to hope she was the forgiving sort.

You've Got to Know What Happens in the Poem

<u>Lines 1-4</u>   He makes blunt, <u>critical statements</u> about his mistress's looks. She doesn't match up to popular ideas of beauty in Elizabethan times, e.g. she's dark-haired, not fair.

<u>Lines 5-12</u>   He lists more beautiful things (roses, music, perfume, goddesses) but then explains that she <u>isn't</u> like any of these either. On line 9, however, it starts to become apparent that <u>he does like her really</u>.

<u>Lines 13-14</u>   In the <u>final rhyming couplet</u>, he says that he thinks his mistress is <u>great</u> — as good as any other woman who's been praised in love poetry.

Learn About the Three Types of Language

1) <u>SUBVERSION OF TRADITIONAL IMAGES OF BEAUTY</u> — Many of the lines sound like they're going to be traditional images of women's beauty. But instead Shakespeare goes <u>against the reader's expectations</u> by saying that his mistress isn't like any of these images.

2) <u>CRITICAL LANGUAGE</u> — He sounds <u>pretty mean</u> about his mistress in the first part of the poem.

3) <u>SONNET FORM</u> — The poem is in traditional sonnet form. It has <u>fourteen lines</u> and is in <u>iambic pentameters</u> (see glossary). Sonnets are often used for <u>love poetry</u>.

Remember the Feelings and Attitudes in the Poem

Time for a hair cut.

1) <u>SUBVERSION</u> — Shakespeare's <u>having fun</u> with this poem, turning the reader's expectations of a love poem on their head.

2) <u>CONTEMPT</u> — He sounds pretty <u>insulting</u> about his mistress's looks, voice and smell in the first part of the poem.

3) <u>LOVE</u> — Then at the end, the message seems to be: "I <u>love her</u> warts and all. I don't need to pretend she's a goddess."

Think About Your Feelings and Attitudes to the Poem

1) Pick 2 words or phrases that <u>stand out to you</u>. If none stand out, just pick 2 <u>unusual words or phrases</u>.

2) Write these 2 words or phrases down. Then write about how they <u>make you feel</u>. If they don't make you feel anything, don't worry — just <u>make something up</u>, as long as it's not too stupid.

> **EXAMPLE**   I really like the phrase "belied with false compare." Often when I read love poetry it does seem pretty false: no one really floats like a goddess or has a voice sweeter than music. The conclusion to this poem is surprisingly down-to-earth and realistic.

Themes — love, imagery and closing couplets...

You can compare this poem with other poems on the same themes: <u>love</u> ('Anne Hathaway' p.40-41), <u>imagery</u> ('Patrolling Barnegat' p.18-19 and 'I've made out a will' p.64-65) and <u>closing couplets</u> ('The Village Schoolmaster' p.28-29 and 'Havisham' p.36-37).

Robert Browning

He's proud of his history and the titles of "Duke" and "Duchess".

He says you shouldn't judge people — but it seems he couldn't help it.

The Duke's jealous — he suggests the Duchess flirted with everyone.

This word suggests he was more bothered about the Duchess's behaviour than he's letting on.

He sounds suspicious of her — maybe he thought she was being unfaithful.

He doesn't explain how this happened, which makes it sound sinister.

Shows his power — but we don't find out what the commands were.

The Duke reminds his visitor of his low status.

He's arranging his next marriage — his Next Duchess.

Moves onto another valuable possession as if he's said nothing unusual.

```
      She rode with round the terrace – all and each
30    Would draw from her alike the approving speech,
      Or blush, at least. She thanked men, – good! but thanked–
      Somehow – I know not how – as if she ranked
      My gift of a nine-hundred-years-old name
      With anybody's gift. Who'd stoop to blame
35    This sort of trifling? Even had you skill
      In speech – (which I have not) – to make your will
      Quite clear to such a one, and say, 'Just this
      'Or that in you disgusts me; here you miss,
      'Or there exceed the mark' – and if she let
40    Herself be lessoned so, nor plainly set
      Her wits to yours, forsooth and made excuse,
      – E'en then would be some stooping; and I choose
      Never to stoop. Oh sir, she smiled, no doubt,
      Whene'er I passed her; but who passed without
45    Much the same smile? This grew; I gave commands;
      Then all smiles stopped together. There she stands
      As if alive. Will't please you to rise? We'll meet
      The company below, then. I repeat,
      The Count your master's known munificence
50    Is ample warrant that no just pretence
      Of mine for dowry will be disallowed;
      Though his fair daughter's self, as I avowed
      At starting, is my object. Nay, we'll go
      Together down, sir. Notice Neptune, though,
55    Taming a sea-horse, thought a rarity,
      Which Claus of Innsbruck cast in bronze for me.
```

POEM DICTIONARY
countenance — face
durst — dare
mantle — cloak
favour — ribbons in the family colours
bough — branch
officious — eager to please
trifling — something that's not important
forsooth — indeed
munificence — generosity
warrant — proof or guarantee
dowry — money paid to a man when he's married
avowed — said
Neptune — Roman god of the sea

Robert Browning

 <u>Robert Browning</u> (1812-1889) was born in Camberwell, Surrey. He read and wrote poems from an early age. He married Elizabeth Barrett, another well-known poet. He produced many collections of poems, before he died in Venice, Italy.

My Last Duchess

Ferrara

> The name of a 16th century Duke.

> Sets a sinister tone.

> Sounds polite, but he's really being quite forceful here.

> He controls who looks at the painting.

> Reference to death is out of place and suspicious.

> The Duke finds it hard to put his irritation into words.

> She was cheery and friendly — but the Duke means this as a criticism.

> The name of the artist.

> The portrait shows she had strong emotions.

> Repeating this shows it bothers him.

> She flirted a lot — the Duke thinks so anyway.

That's my last Duchess painted on the wall,
Looking as if she were alive. I call
That piece a wonder, now: Frà Pandolf's hands
Worked busily a day, and there she stands.
5 Will't please you sit and look at her? I said
'Frà Pandolf' by design, for never read
Strangers like you that pictured countenance,
The depth and passion of its earnest glance,
But to myself they turned (since none puts by
10 The curtain I have drawn for you, but I)
And seemed as they would ask me, if they durst
How such a glance came there; so, not the first
Are you to turn and ask thus. Sir, 'twas not
Her husband's presence only, called that spot
15 Of joy into the Duchess' cheek: perhaps
Frà Pandolf chanced to say 'Her mantle laps
'Over my lady's wrist too much,' or 'Paint
'Must never hope to reproduce the faint
'Half-flush that dies along her throat:' such stuff
20 Was courtesy, she thought, and cause enough
For calling up that spot of joy. She had
A heart — how shall I say? — too soon made glad,
Too easily impressed; she liked whate'er
She looked on, and her looks went everywhere.
25 Sir, 'twas all one! My favour at her breast,
The dropping of the daylight in the West,
The bough of cherries some officious fool
Broke in the orchard for her, the white mule

THIS IS A FLAP.
FOLD THIS PAGE OUT.

My Last Duchess

In this poem, a Duke is talking to a visitor about a <u>portrait</u> of his wife, who is now dead. He says he really likes the picture, but then he goes on about how she used to <u>smile</u> and have a laugh with everyone, and this annoyed him. We begin to suspect her death may have been a bit <u>suspicious</u>.

You've Got to Know What Happens in the Poem

<u>Lines 1-5</u>	The Duke points out the <u>portrait</u> of the Duchess to a visitor. He's very <u>proud</u> of it.
<u>Lines 5-13</u>	He says people always ask him about the <u>passionate expression</u> on the Duchess's face.
<u>Lines 13-21</u>	The Duke says the Duchess's flirty expression <u>wasn't</u> reserved <u>just for him</u>.
<u>Lines 21-34</u>	He says she <u>smiled at everyone</u>. He's annoyed that she treated him just like <u>anyone else</u>.
<u>Lines 34-43</u>	He says it would have been <u>wrong</u> to <u>criticise</u> her for her behaviour.
<u>Lines 43-47</u>	He acted to <u>stop</u> the Duchess's <u>flirting</u> — but, suspiciously, he doesn't say <u>how</u> he did this.
<u>Lines 47-56</u>	The Duke and his guest <u>walk away</u> from the painting. The Duke reveals he's planning to get <u>married again</u>, this time to the daughter of a Count.

Learn About the Three Types of Language

1) <u>JEALOUS LANGUAGE</u> — The things the Duke says about the Duchess sound quite innocent at first. But we can read <u>hidden meanings</u> into them which hint at the Duke's <u>jealousy</u>, e.g. by saying she <u>smiled</u> a lot, he seems to suggest that she was a <u>flirt</u>, and maybe <u>unfaithful</u> to him.

2) <u>SINISTER LANGUAGE</u> — The Duke sometimes says things that make him sound a bit <u>sinister</u> — there's a <u>dark side</u> to him. We begin to suspect that he might have <u>killed</u> the Duchess.

3) <u>LANGUAGE ABOUT POWER</u> — The Duke feels the need to have <u>power</u> and <u>control</u> over the Duchess. He sees her as another of his <u>possessions</u>, just like his expensive paintings.

Remember the Feelings and Attitudes in the Poem

"The brazen hussy..."

1) <u>PRIDE</u> — The Duke is very proud of his <u>possessions</u> and his <u>status</u>.

2) <u>JEALOUSY</u> — He <u>couldn't stand</u> the way the Duchess treated him <u>no better</u> than anyone else (lines 31-34).

3) <u>POWER</u> — The Duke enjoys the <u>control</u> he has over the painting (lines 9-10). He didn't have this power over the Duchess when she was alive.

Think About Your Feelings and Attitudes to the Poem

1) Pick 2 words or phrases that <u>stand out to you</u>. If none stand out, just pick 2 <u>unusual words or phrases</u>.

2) Write these 2 words or phrases down. Then write about how they <u>make you feel</u>. If they don't make you feel anything, don't worry — just <u>make something up</u>, as long as it's not too stupid.

> **EXAMPLE** When the Duke says "all smiles stopped together", I'm very suspicious of him. His tone suggests he was satisfied with the result of his "commands". As the Duchess is now dead, this seems rather sinister to me.

Themes — attitudes towards others, evil and first person...

You should compare this poem with other poems about the same themes: <u>attitudes towards other people</u> ('Havisham' p.36-37), <u>evil</u> ('The Laboratory' p.30-31 and 'Education for Leisure' p.48-49) and <u>use of first person</u> ('Elvis's Twin Sister' p.38-39 and 'Hitcher' p.66-67).

Alfred Tennyson

Alfred Tennyson (1809-1892) was born in Lincolnshire and later lived on the Isle of Wight and in Surrey. He studied at Trinity College, Cambridge. Tennyson was one of the great poets of the Victorian era and was Poet Laureate from 1850 to 1892.

Alliteration — the harsh "c" sound emphasises the toughness of the eagle and his surroundings.

Strong, determined grip.

The poet describes the eagle as "he", not "it".

Surrounded by a vast emptiness.

Shows how high the eagle's position is.

Personification — the eagle is described as an old man.

Far away and alone.

He seems to be waiting.

The sea looks slow and tame from where he is.

Like a house. The eagle owns the mountain.

Contrast with the end of the first verse. The two sides of the eagle are shown — first waiting, then acting.

Simile shows the eagle's incredible natural power and speed.

The Eagle

He clasps the crag with crookèd hands;
Close to the sun in lonely lands,
Ring'd with the azure world, he stands.

The wrinkled sea beneath him crawls;
5   He watches from his mountain walls,
And like a thunderbolt he falls.

POEM DICTIONARY
azure — blue

The Eagle

The poet describes a magnificent <u>eagle</u>. That's it.

You've Got to Know What Happens in the Poem

<u>Lines 1-3</u>   The eagle stands on a <u>cliff</u>, in front of the sun and surrounded by the big blue <u>sky</u>.

<u>Lines 4-6</u>   The eagle patiently watches the <u>sea</u>, then <u>dives</u> into it for food, quick as a flash.

> Lines 1-3 show how great the eagle looks just <u>standing there</u>.
> Lines 4-6 show how good he looks <u>in action</u>.

Learn About the Three Types of Language

1) <u>PERSONIFICATION</u> — The poet describes the eagle as if it's a <u>person</u> he respects — e.g. he says "him" rather than "it". The eagle is like an admirable <u>old man</u>.

2) <u>ISOLATION</u> — The eagle is <u>alone</u> and <u>unique</u>. He belongs to the <u>sky</u> around him, not the earth way below.

3) <u>POWERFUL LANGUAGE</u> — The eagle is <u>strong</u> and <u>fast</u>. He's the king of everything he sees.

Remember the Feelings and Attitudes in the Poem

"Here, fishy-fishy..."

1) <u>RESPECT</u> — The poet <u>respects</u> the magnificent <u>strong figure</u> of the eagle perched on the cliff.

2) <u>ADMIRATION</u> — He also <u>admires</u> the physical <u>speed</u> and <u>power</u> of the eagle when he dives towards the sea.

Think About Your Feelings and Attitudes to the Poem

1) Pick 2 words or phrases that <u>stand out to you</u>. If none stand out, just pick 2 <u>unusual words or phrases</u>.

2) Write these 2 words or phrases down. Then write about how they <u>make you feel</u>. If they don't make you feel anything, don't worry — just <u>make something up</u>, as long as it's not too stupid.

> **EXAMPLE** The simile "like a thunderbolt" makes me feel amazed at the eagle's speed. His dive happens in a flash, almost too quick to see, but also with great power.

Themes — language effects and imagery...

Compare 'The Eagle' with other poems about the same themes: <u>language effects</u> ('Inversnaid' p.32-33, 'Sonnet' p.34-35 and 'Stealing' p.50-51) and <u>imagery</u> 'The Little Boy Lost'/'The Little Boy Found' p.12-13, 'Elvis's Twin Sister' p.38-39 and 'Homecoming' p.56-57).

Alfred Tennyson

The seas are dark and scary.

He reminds his crew of their past achievements.

> There lies in the port; the vessel puffs her sail:
> 45 There gloom the dark broad seas. My mariners,
>   Souls that have toiled, and wrought, and thought with me –
>   That ever was a frolic welcome took
>   The thunder and the sunshine, and opposed
>   Free hearts, free foreheads – you and I are old;
> 50 Old age hath yet his honour and his toil;
>   Death closes all: but something ere the end,
>   Some work of noble note, may yet be done,
>   Not unbecoming men that strove with Gods.
>   The lights begin to twinkle from the rocks:
> 55 The long day wanes: the slow moon climbs: the deep
>   Moans round with many voices. Come, my friends,
>   'Tis not too late to seek a newer world.
>   Push off, and sitting well in order smite
>   The sounding furrows; for my purpose holds
> 60 To sail beyond the sunset, and the baths
>   Of all the western stars, until I die.
>   It may be that the gulfs will wash us down:
>   It may be we shall touch the Happy Isles,
>   And see the great Achilles, whom we knew.
> 65 Though much is taken, much abides; and though
>   We are not now that strength which in old days
>   Moved earth and heaven; that which we are, we are;
>   One equal temper of heroic hearts,
>   Made weak by time and fate, but strong in will
> 70 To strive, to seek, to find and not to yield.

He's realistic — just because he's a hero, he doesn't think he's invincible.

He reminds his crew that they don't have much time left in life.

He feels the sea is calling him away.

Talks to the seamen as his equals.

Another reminder that death isn't far away.

He tells his band of men that they're a good team.

Ulysses ends his speech with a flourish, to motivate his crew.

POEM DICTIONARY

Ulysses — Roman name for Odysseus, a Greek hero, who fought
    in the Trojan War and spent ten years travelling home
mete and dole — give out
lees — last drops
scudding — moving quickly, as in a storm
vext — angered
unburnished — unpolished
Telemachus — son of Ulysses
discerning — showing judgement
sceptre — symbol of ruling power
prudence — care, caution

mariners — sailors
wrought — worked
frolic — light-hearted
ere — before
unbecoming — unsuitable
strove — fought
wanes — draws to a close
smite — strike
furrows — trenches
Achilles — another Greek hero
abides — stays

Alfred Tennyson

Ulysses

It little profits that an idle king,
By this still hearth, among these barren crags,
Matched with an agèd wife, I mete and dole
Unequal laws unto a savage race,
5   That hoard, and sleep, and feed, and know not me.
I cannot rest from travel: I will drink
Life to the lees: all times I have enjoyed
Greatly, have suffered greatly, both with those
That loved me, and alone; on shore, and when
10 Through scudding drifts the rainy Hyades
Vext the dim sea; I am become a name;
For always roaming with a hungry heart
Much have I seen and known; cities of men
And manners, climates, councils, governments,
15 Myself not least, but honoured of them all;
And drunk delight of battle with my peers,
Far on the ringing plains of windy Troy.
I am a part of all that I have met;
Yet all experience is an arch wherethrough
20 Gleams that untravelled world, whose margin fades
For ever and for ever when I move.
How dull it is to pause, to make an end,
To rust unburnished, not to shine in use!
As though to breathe were life. Life piled on life
25 Were all too little, and of one to me
Little remains: but every hour is saved
From that eternal silence, something more,
A bringer of new things; and vile it were
For some three suns to store and hoard myself,
30 And to this gray spirit yearning in desire
To follow knowledge like a sinking star,
Beyond the utmost bound of human thought.

This is my son, mine own Telemachus,
To whom I leave the sceptre and the isle –
35 Well-loved of me, discerning to fulfil
This labour, by slow prudence to make mild
A rugged people, and through soft degrees
Subdue them to the useful and the good.
Most blameless is he, centred in the sphere
40 Of common duties, decent not to fail
In offices of tenderness, and pay
Meet adoration to my household gods,
When I am gone. He works his work, I mine.

Annotations

Down-to-earth setting.

The plodding rhythm in this verse reflects his boredom and frustration.

This sums up his attitude.

He's determined to use up every last second of life.

He knows he's famous.

He's proud and confident.

Alliteration adds to the sense of eagerness.

Describes how warriors become drunk with the excitement of battle.

The ancient city where the Trojan War was fought.

Each adventure makes you realise how many more adventures there are out there.

He feels useless and bored when he's resting.

Compares himself to a sword, rusting through lack of use.

He doesn't have enough time left to do all the things he wants to do.

He's desperate for new experiences.

He wants to carry on travelling forever — his journey will never be complete.

His son's boring duties contrast with the excitement of Ulysses' adventures.

He's going on a voyage but also facing up to death.

He and his son are different kinds of people.

THIS IS A FLAP.
FOLD THIS PAGE OUT.

Ulysses

This poem is about the ancient Greek hero <u>Ulysses</u>. He's returned from the Trojan War to rule his home island of Ithaca as King — but he feels restless. He decides he needs to spend the rest of his life having <u>more adventures</u>. The poem ends with a motivating speech to his crew.

You've Got to Know What Happens in the Poem

<u>Lines 1-5</u>   Ulysses has returned home. He feels <u>frustrated</u> and <u>bored</u> ruling his "savage" people.

<u>Lines 6-32</u>   He decides he has to <u>continue his adventures</u> right up to his dying day. He remembers his past adventures and says there's <u>no point</u> in just sitting about — he has to get all he can out of life.

<u>Lines 33-43</u>   He talks about his <u>son</u>, Telemachus. He says Telemachus is less adventurous, but he'll make a <u>good ruler</u>, and Ulysses is proud of him — but he's a <u>different</u> kind of person from Ulysses.

<u>Lines 44-61</u>   Ulysses addresses his <u>crew</u> before they set off on their voyage. He says that he and they may be <u>old</u>, but they're brave and strong men who are still capable of new <u>achievements</u>.

<u>Lines 62-70</u>   Ulysses <u>motivates his crew</u>. He tells them that they're not as strong as they once were, and they may not come back alive, but they're <u>brave men</u> who will give their all.

Learn About the Four Types of Language

1)   <u>HEROIC LANGUAGE</u> — Ulysses proudly describes his exciting <u>adventures</u>.
He uses stirring, heroic language to <u>fire up</u> his crew before their next voyage.

2)   <u>IMAGERY</u> — Ulysses creates some <u>powerful images</u> of his battles and adventures.

3)   <u>LANGUAGE ABOUT DEATH</u> — He knows that he's <u>old</u>, and this makes him determined to <u>get the most</u> out of the time he has left. He mentions <u>death</u> several times, but he doesn't seem scared of dying.

4)   <u>LANGUAGE ABOUT FRUSTRATION</u> — He feels <u>bored</u> and <u>frustrated</u> when he's not active.

Remember the Feelings and Attitudes in the Poem

1)   <u>BOREDOM</u> — Ulysses feels <u>bored</u> by the thought of ruling his people at home. He seems <u>scornful</u> of them: "a savage race".

2)   <u>PRIDE</u> — Ulysses is <u>proud</u> of his brave reputation and his great achievements in the past.

3)   <u>EXCITEMENT</u> — He <u>looks forward</u> to the coming voyage and uses his own excitement to <u>inspire</u> his crew.

Think About Your Feelings and Attitudes to the Poem

1)   Pick 2 words or phrases that <u>stand out to you</u>. If none stand out, just pick 2 <u>unusual words or phrases</u>.

2)   Write these 2 words or phrases down. Then write about how they <u>make you feel</u>. If they don't make you feel anything, don't worry — just <u>make something up</u>, as long as it's not too stupid.

> **EXAMPLE**   I really respect Ulysses' courage when he says "my purpose holds / To sail beyond the sunset". This line shows he is determined to continue his adventures for as long as possible, and he is not afraid of death.

Themes — death, memory and getting older...

You could compare 'Ulysses' with other poems about the same themes: <u>death</u> ('Tichborne's Elegy p.14-15, 'The Man He Killed' p.16-17 and 'November' p.58-59), <u>memory</u> ('The Village Schoolmaster p.28-29) and <u>getting older</u> ('November' p.58-59 and 'Kid' p.60-61).

Oliver Goldsmith

<u>Oliver Goldsmith</u> (1730-1774) was an Irish playwright and poet. He studied at Trinity College, Dublin. He was also a translator and wrote children's books and histories.

The Village Schoolmaster

Images of the countryside.

There are rhyming couplets all the way through.

Describing the school like this shows he was in charge.

It doesn't sound like he was much fun.

The children were frightened of him.

He took his bad moods out on other people.

The pupils pretended to find his jokes funny to keep him in a good mood.

If he was severe, it was because he liked studying so much.

Sounds like they were scared of his temper.

There were rumours about him, which suggests no-one knew him all that well.

He had an impressive range of skills.

He was stubborn — he'd carry on arguing even when he was wrong.

Suggests he had a loud voice.

Fairly disrespectful way of describing the schoolmaster — the adults weren't scared of him.

He was an outsider. The villagers didn't know what to make of him.

He was very knowledgeable.

Beside yon straggling fence that skirts the way,
With blossomed furze unprofitably gay,
There, in his noisy mansion, skilled to rule,
The village master taught his little school;
5 A man severe he was, and stern to view,
I knew him well, and every truant knew;
Well had the boding tremblers learned to trace
The day's disasters in his morning face;
Full well they laughed, with counterfeited glee,
10 At all his jokes, for many a joke had he:
Full well the busy whisper, circling round,
Conveyed the dismal tidings when he frowned;
Yet he was kind, or, if severe in aught,
The love he bore to learning was in fault;
15 The village all declared how much he knew;
'Twas certain he could write, and cipher too;
Lands he could measure, terms and tides presage,
And even the story ran that he could gauge.
In arguing, too, the parson owned his skill,
20 For, even though vanquished, he could argue still;
While words of learned length and thundering sound
Amazed the gazing rustics ranged around;
And still they gazed, and still the wonder grew
That one small head could carry all he knew.

<u>POEM DICTIONARY</u>
furze — gorse bush
boding — predicting
counterfeited — faked
conveyed — told
tidings — news
aught — anything
cipher — count, do arithmetic
presage — forecast
gauge — measure
vanquished — defeated
rustics — people who live in the countryside

The Village Schoolmaster

This poem is about the old <u>schoolmaster</u> of a village school. He was a rather strange bloke — he was bad-tempered and a bit <u>frightening</u>, but also very <u>intelligent</u> and skilful. Although the poet doesn't say it outright, it seems that the people in the village thought he was a bit of a weirdo.

You've Got to Know *What Happens in the Poem*

<u>Lines 1-12</u>	The poet points out a place in the <u>countryside</u> where a village school was. Then we hear about how <u>strict</u> the schoolmaster was — he was often in a <u>bad mood</u> and the pupils were <u>scared</u> of him.
<u>Lines 13-24</u>	Then the poet says how <u>clever</u> the schoolmaster was. He had loads of different <u>skills</u>. The villagers were <u>amazed</u> by how much he knew — although they didn't seem to like him very much.

Learn About the *Three Types of Language*

1) <u>INTIMIDATING LANGUAGE</u> — The way the schoolmaster looked and acted makes him seem <u>scary</u> and <u>unpleasant</u>. The children were afraid of his <u>temper</u>, and laughed at his rubbish jokes to avoid getting on the wrong side of him.

2) <u>LANGUAGE ABOUT EDUCATION</u> — The schoolmaster had all sorts of <u>skills</u> and <u>knowledge</u>. The villagers were <u>amazed</u> at how much he knew.

3) <u>MYSTERY</u> — He was an <u>outsider</u> and a <u>loner</u>. The people in the village didn't know much about him and seemed to think he was a bit <u>odd</u>, rather than respecting him.

Remember the Feelings and Attitudes *in the Poem*

"Today, children, you're going to learn about how great I am."

1) <u>FEAR</u> — The children were <u>scared</u> of the schoolmaster.

2) <u>FASCINATION</u> — The villagers were <u>fascinated</u> by the schoolmaster, but they <u>didn't respect</u> him very much (lines 23-24).

3) <u>MOCKERY</u> — The poet seems to <u>mock</u> the school master — he suggests he's a <u>pompous show-off</u> (although he doesn't openly say this).

Think About *Your Feelings and Attitudes to the Poem*

1) Pick 2 words or phrases that <u>stand out to you</u>. If none stand out, just pick 2 <u>unusual words or phrases</u>.

2) Write these 2 words or phrases down. Then write about how they <u>make you feel</u>. If they don't make you feel anything, don't worry — just <u>make something up</u>, as long as it's not too stupid.

> **EXAMPLE** The description of the schoolmaster as having "The day's disasters in his morning face" makes him sound scary and intimidating. I wouldn't want to have him as my headteacher.

Themes — *characters, closing couplets, memory...*

Compare 'The Village Schoolmaster' with other poems on the same themes: <u>characters</u> ('Ulysses' p.26-27 and 'Kid' p.60-61), <u>closing couplets</u> ('Havisham' p.36-37 and 'I've made out a will' p.64-65) and <u>memory</u> ('We Remember Your Childhood Well' p.46-47 and 'Homecoming' p.56-57).

Robert Browning

VII

25 Quick—is it finished? The colour's too grim!
Why not soft like the phial's, enticing and dim?
Let it brighten her drink, let her turn it and stir,
And try it and taste, ere she fix and prefer!

She has the whole plan worked out, down to the smallest details.

She's worried there's not enough poison.

VIII

What a drop! She's not little, no minion like me!
30 That's why she ensnared him: this never will free
The soul from those masculine eyes,—say, 'no!'
That to pulse's magnificent come-and-go.

She says her lover's mistress trapped him.

Respectful way of describing life — but she wants to end it.

IX

For only last night, as they whispered, I brought
My own eyes to bear on her so, that I thought
35 Could I keep them one half minute fixed, she would fall
Shrivelled; she fell not; yet this does it all!

Graphic description of death.

X

Not that I bid you spare her the pain;
Let death be felt and the proof remain:
Brand, burn up, bite into its grace—
40 He is sure to remember her dying face!

She wants the mistress to suffer — she wants absolute revenge.

She enjoys the cruelty of what she's doing.

XI

Is it done? Take my mask off! Nay, be not morose;
It kills her, and this prevents seeing it close:
The delicate droplet, my whole fortune's fee!
If it hurts her, beside, can it ever hurt me?

She's so keen to see the poison, she risks removing her protective mask.

The poison is her most valuable possession.

XII

45 Now, take all my jewels, gorge gold to your fill,
You may kiss me, old man, on my mouth if you will!
But brush this dust off me, lest horror it brings
Ere I know it—next moment I dance at the King's!

She spends everything she has on the poison.

She's delighted that the poison is ready.

POEM DICTIONARY

thy — your	signet — a seal on a ring
thou — you	filigree — delicate ornamental metal
pliest — carry out	lozenge — a tablet or pill
smithy — workshop	pastile — a substance burnt to clean the air
prithee — please	enticing — tempting
drear — dreary	ere — before
mortar — a small bowl	minion — a small, weak person
whence — from where	ensnared — trapped
yonder — over there	Brand — mark painfully
phial — a small bottle	morose — sad
thee — you	gorge — eat greedily
casket — a small box for jewels	lest — in case

Robert Browning

The Laboratory

ANCIEN RÉGIME

This tells us that the poem is set in France, in the days when they had kings and queens.

I

She wears a mask for safety.

Now that I, tying thy glass mask tightly,
May gaze thro' these faint smokes curling whitely,

She knows what she's doing is evil.

As thou pliest thy trade in this devil's-smithy—
Which is the poison to poison her, prithee?

II

She thinks everyone's laughing at her — this makes her more determined to get revenge.

5   He is with her, and they know that I know
Where they are, what they do: they believe my tears flow

The whole poem is in rhyming couplets.

While they laugh, laugh at me, at me fled to the drear
Empty church, to pray God in, for them! —I am here.

III

The way she describes making the poison shows her violent feelings.

Grind away, moisten and mash up thy paste,

10   Pound at thy powder,—I am not in haste!

Their lives are based around the Royal Court.

Better sit thus, and observe thy strange things,
Than go where men wait me and dance at the King's.

IV

She wants to know how the poison is made, and where the ingredients come from.

That in the mortar—you call it a gum?

The poison is precious to her.

Ah, the brave tree whence such gold oozings come!

15   And yonder soft phial, the exquisite blue,
Sure to taste sweetly,—is that poison too?

The colour of the poison is beautiful to her.

V

Had I but all of them, thee and thy treasures,

The potions are rare and valuable.

What a wild crowd of invisible pleasures!

There's no doubt about what she wants to happen.

To carry pure death in an earring, a casket,

20   A signet, a fan-mount, a filigree basket!

She gets carried away with excitement, listing all the things she can think of that could hold poison.

VI

There's a dark humour here — usually people would use these to make things better.

Soon, at the King's, a mere lozenge to give,
And Pauline should have just thirty minutes to live!
But to light a pastile, and Elise, with her head
And her breast and her arms and her hands, should drop dead!

The idea of killing excites her.

THIS IS A FLAP.
FOLD THIS PAGE OUT.

The Laboratory

This poem's set in France back in the days when they had a monarchy. A rich woman is buying some <u>poison</u> so that she can <u>kill</u> a woman who is having an affair with her lover/husband (it's not clear who exactly the man is). Seems a trifle extreme...

You've Got to Know What Happens in the Poem

<u>Lines 1-4</u>	The woman talks to the chemist while he <u>mixes the poison</u> in his workshop.
<u>Lines 5-8</u>	Her lover is with <u>another woman</u> and they think she's <u>at church</u> crying — but she's not.
<u>Lines 9-20</u>	She watches the chemist and says how <u>lovely</u> the <u>poisons</u> look. She wants <u>all of them</u>.
<u>Lines 21-24</u>	She plans to <u>poison two other women</u> called Pauline and Elise at the King's Court.
<u>Lines 25-28</u>	She tells the chemist to make the poison <u>brighter</u>, to make her lover's mistress drink it.
<u>Lines 29-32</u>	She says there's <u>not enough</u> poison to kill the mistress — she's too big and strong.
<u>Lines 33-40</u>	Last night, she felt she could <u>kill</u> the mistress by <u>looking</u> at her. She wants her to die <u>painfully</u>.
<u>Lines 41-48</u>	She's so <u>grateful</u> to the chemist she offers to kiss him. Now she's off to <u>use the poison</u>.

Learn About the Three Types of Language

1) <u>VIOLENT LANGUAGE</u> — She's absolutely <u>merciless</u> about taking her revenge. She wants the mistress's death to be <u>horrible</u> and <u>painful</u>, and violent thoughts are never far from her mind.

2) <u>IMAGERY</u> — For all her nastiness, she uses quite <u>fancy</u> language in her descriptions.

3) <u>OBSESSIVE LANGUAGE</u> — She gives up all her <u>wealth</u> and <u>possessions</u> for the poison — <u>nothing else matters</u> to her. She gets very <u>excited</u> when she thinks about revenge.

Remember the Feelings and Attitudes in the Poem

Ice with your poison, I mean drink?

1) <u>OBSESSION</u> — She's <u>obsessed</u> with the thought of getting <u>revenge</u>.
2) <u>SINGLE-MINDEDNESS</u> — revenge is all that matters to her.
3) <u>IMMORALITY</u> — She knows what she's doing is <u>wrong</u>, but she <u>doesn't care</u>.

> She wants to kill the mistress just to get revenge on her lover/husband for being unfaithful — pretty twisted really.

Think About Your Feelings and Attitudes to the Poem

1) Pick 2 words or phrases that <u>stand out to you</u>. If none stand out, just pick 2 <u>unusual words or phrases</u>.
2) Write these 2 words or phrases down. Then write about how they <u>make you feel</u>. If they don't make you feel anything, don't worry — just <u>make something up</u>, as long as it's not too stupid.

> **EXAMPLE** I am horrified by the line "He is sure to remember her dying face!". She wants her lover to see his mistress when she dies, which is a very sick way of getting revenge on him.

Themes — evil, danger, characters...

Compare 'The Laboratory' with other poems on the same themes: <u>evil</u> ('Education for Leisure' p.48-49), <u>danger</u> ('Hitcher' p.66-67) and <u>characters</u> ('Havisham' p.36-37, 'Salome' p.42-43 and 'Those bastards in their mansions' p.62-63).

Gerard Manley Hopkins

<u>Gerard Manley Hopkins</u> (1844-1889) was born in Stratford, Essex. He studied Classics at Balliol College, Oxford, and was a famous Victorian poet. He became a Jesuit priest and concentrated on teaching and preaching for several years, before resuming his writing.

Inversnaid

> This darksome burn, horseback brown,
> His rollrock highroad roaring down,
> In coop and in comb the fleece of his foam
> Flutes and low to the lake falls home.
>
> 5   A windpuff-bonnet of fawn-froth
> Turns and twindles over the broth
> Of a pool so pitchblack, fell-frowning,
> It rounds and rounds Despair to drowning.
>
> Degged with dew, dappled with dew
> 10 Are the groins of the braes that the brook treads through,
> Wiry heathpacks, flitches of fern,
> And the beadbonny ash that sits over the burn.
>
> What would the world be, once bereft
> Of wet and of wildness? Let them be left,
> 15 O let them be left, wildness and wet;
> Long live the weeds and the wilderness yet.

Annotations:

- Repetition of how dark the stream is.
- Alliteration of "c" sounds makes the stream sound rough.
- Constant movement, like a whirlpool.
- Alliteration and repetition shows that there's dew all around.
- The tree doesn't move but it's alive.
- Alliteration of "r" sounds suggests the roar of water.
- The bubbles of the stream are described like they're a person's or animal's hair.
- The froth is like a hat on the water.
- Hostile and unwelcoming.
- The stream moves like a person walking.
- Repetition gives a passionate, emotional feel.
- "W" sounds are repeated throughout this verse.

<u>POEM DICTIONARY</u>
burn — stream
coop — an enclosed area
comb — the top of a wave
fawn — light greyish-brown colour
fell — fiercely
degged — sprinkled
dappled — spotted
braes — hills
flitches — cuttings
bereft — deprived

Inversnaid

This poem is about a burn (stream) flowing through a rugged, unspoilt area of Scotland. The area is <u>wild</u> and <u>beautiful</u>, and the poet wants it to stay that way. Don't we all, Gerard...

You've Got to Know What Happens in the Poem

<u>Lines 1-4</u>	A dark-coloured <u>stream</u> flows down into a lake.
<u>Lines 5-8</u>	The stream sounds <u>dark</u> and <u>angry</u>.
<u>Lines 9-12</u>	There's <u>dew</u> on the hills, some <u>wild plants</u>, and an <u>ash tree</u> by the river.
<u>Lines 13-16</u>	The poet says we should <u>leave</u> beautiful places like this <u>as they are</u>.

Learn About the Three Types of Language

1) <u>SOUND EFFECTS</u> — There's loads of <u>alliteration</u> to create the effect of the fast flow of water. There's also plenty of <u>rhyming</u>, <u>assonance</u> and <u>onomatopoeia</u> (see glossary, p.92) to help us feel like we can really hear the sounds of the country. These effects add to the rugged, natural feel.

2) <u>PERSONIFICATION</u> — The burn is described as if it's a <u>person</u>. This allows the poet to make it sound angry and fierce, and also <u>strong</u> and <u>admirable</u>.

3) <u>EMOTIONAL LANGUAGE</u> — The poet feels <u>passionately</u> that places like this should be left alone. He seems to be <u>worried</u> that the growth of towns and cities means there are <u>fewer and fewer</u> unspoilt areas of countryside.

Remember the Feelings and Attitudes in the Poem

Something's not right...

1) <u>DANGER</u> — The stream seems <u>fierce</u> and <u>dangerous</u>.
2) <u>BEAUTY</u> — The whole area is <u>beautiful</u>, <u>rugged</u> and <u>unspoilt</u>.
3) <u>PRESERVATION</u> — The poet wants this place to stay as it is. He believes it would be <u>terrible</u> if beautiful, natural places like this <u>didn't exist</u> any more.

Think About Your Feelings and Attitudes to the Poem

1) Pick 2 words or phrases that <u>stand out to you</u>. If none stand out, just pick 2 <u>unusual words or phrases</u>.
2) Write these 2 words or phrases down. Then write about how they <u>make you feel</u>. If they don't make you feel anything, don't worry — just <u>make something up</u>, as long as it's not too stupid.

> **EXAMPLE** When the poet asks "What would the world be, once bereft / Of wet and of wildness?", it makes me sad. I live in a city, a long way from anywhere like the place the poet describes, and I think it is a pity that so many people grow up without knowing places like this.

Themes — imagery, mood, language effects...

Compare this poem with other poems on the same themes: <u>imagery</u> ('Sonnet' p.34-35 and 'Homecoming' p.56-57), <u>mood</u> ('Elvis's Twin Sister' p.38-39 and 'November' p.58-59) and <u>language effects</u> ('Sonnet 130' p.20-21 and 'Stealing' p.50-51).

John Clare

John Clare (1793-1864) was the son of a Northampton labourer. He left school at 11 and educated himself after that. For most of his life he lived in rural Northamptonshire. He is famous for writing poems about life in the country, although he also wrote about politics, the environment, corruption and poverty.

> Repetition emphasises his feelings.

> The soft, fluffy clouds are like wool.

> Gold and white colours show the brightness of early summer.

> Trees around the lake make it seem alive and healthy.

> Natural and unspoilt.

> The insects are playful and fun-loving.

> Alliteration

> The whole scene is shining brightly.

> Rhyming couplets throughout the poem.

> Gentle movement.

> Brightness continues to the end of the poem.

> The poem finishes on a light-hearted, carefree note.

Sonnet

I love to see the summer beaming forth
And white wool sack clouds sailing to the north
I love to see the wild flowers come again
And Mare blobs stain with gold the meadow drain
5   And water lilies whiten on the floods
Where reed clumps rustle like a wind shook wood
Where from her hiding place the Moor Hen pushes
And seeks her flag nest floating in bull rushes
I like the willow leaning half way o'er
10   The clear deep lake to stand upon its shore
I love the hay grass when the flower head swings
To summer winds and insects happy wings
That sport about the meadow the bright day
And see bright beetles in the clear lake play

POEM DICTIONARY
sonnet — a poem with 14 lines
Mare blobs — buttercups
Moor Hen — a bird that lives on ponds
flag — type of leaf
bull rushes — plants that grow in ponds
o'er — over

Sonnet

This is a good old-fashioned poem about how lovely <u>summer</u> in the countryside is. It's a really <u>idealistic</u> poem — the poet talks about all the <u>best</u> things in summer, like pretty flowers, trees and meadows (and ignores things like hayfever and another dull series of Big Brother).

You've Got to Know What Happens in the Poem

Lines 1-4   The poet describes how much he likes the <u>lovely summer</u>, with the <u>lovely clouds</u> floating over the <u>lovely flowers</u> in the <u>lovely meadow</u>.

Lines 5-10   Lilies and reeds grow in the <u>lake</u>. A bird swims across the water. The poet says how great the <u>willow trees</u> on the banks are.

Lines 11-14   He says he loves the way the <u>grass</u> and <u>flowers</u> blow in the <u>wind</u>, and cheery little <u>insects</u> skip about on the surface of the lake.

Learn About the Two Types of Language

1)   <u>VISUAL LANGUAGE</u> — <u>Nature</u> is in full bloom. The <u>sun</u> is out, the fields are <u>golden</u> — even the <u>beetles</u> are bright...

2)   <u>PEACEFULNESS</u> — The countryside is quiet and calm. The <u>flowers</u> are swaying in the gentle breeze. The insects are just messing around and <u>not stinging</u> anyone. It's a very <u>idealistic</u> poem.

> There's <u>no punctuation</u> in the poem. This helps the poet to create one big image, made up of all the different things he describes.

Remember the Feelings and Attitudes in the Poem

Ah, the glorious British summer of 2004.

1)   <u>LOVE</u> — He <u>loves</u> the summer and the natural scenery.

2)   <u>TRANQUILLITY</u> — He feels <u>relaxed</u> and <u>at peace</u>.

3)   <u>HAPPINESS</u> — Overall, he's just dead <u>happy</u> that it's summer and he's in the countryside. Bless.

Think About Your Feelings and Attitudes to the Poem

1)   Pick 2 words or phrases that <u>stand out to you</u>. If none stand out, just pick 2 <u>unusual words or phrases</u>.

2)   Write these 2 words or phrases down. Then write about how they <u>make you feel</u>. If they don't make you feel anything, don't worry — just <u>make something up</u>, as long as it's not too stupid.

> **EXAMPLE**   The phrase "summer beaming forth" reminds me of the long summer holidays when I was really young. The whole world seemed to be bright and blooming, and this poem brings back the happy, relaxed feelings of that time for me.

Themes — language effects, mood, imagery...

You could compare 'Sonnet' with other poems on the same themes: <u>language effects</u> ('The Eagle' p.24-25 and 'Anne Hathaway' p.40-41), <u>mood</u> ('Inversnaid' p.32-33) and <u>imagery</u> ('Before You Were Mine' p.44-45 and 'My father thought it bloody queer' p.54-55).

Havisham

Carol Ann Duffy was born in 1955 in Glasgow. She studied philosophy at the University of Liverpool, and in 1996 began lecturing in poetry at Manchester Metropolitan University. As well as writing poetry, she has also written plays.

Her feelings are a confused mix — the tender love she would have had for him as a husband, and her violent bitterness at being rejected.

Havisham

She's become so hardened by her hatred that she can't see clearly.

Beloved sweetheart bastard. Not a day since then
I haven't wished him dead. Prayed for it
so hard I've dark green pebbles for eyes,
ropes on the back of my hands I could strangle with.

She's so angry she could use her veins to strangle him.

She's disgusted with herself too.

She screams like an animal.

5   Spinster. I stink and remember. Whole days
in bed cawing Nooooo at the wall; the dress
yellowing, trembling if I open the wardrobe;
the slewed mirror, full-length, her, myself, who did this

She wonders how she's become so messed up.

This shows us how long she's been wearing her wedding dress.

to me? Puce curses that are sounds not words.
10   Some nights better, the lost body over me,
my fluent tongue in its mouth in its ear
then down till I suddenly bite awake. Love's

She recognises how irrational and wild she's become.

Even her dreams end violently.

The veil usually hides a bride, but here it hides her hatred.

hate behind a white veil; a red balloon bursting
in my face. Bang. I stabbed at a wedding-cake.
15   Give me a male corpse for a long slow honeymoon.
Don't think it's only the heart that b-b-b-breaks.

Usually a happy time, but here it's connected with death and revenge.

Any man will do — she wants revenge on men in general.

POEM DICTIONARY
Havisham — Miss Havisham is a character in 'Great Expectations' by Charles Dickens.
          She was abandoned by her fiancé on her wedding day.
spinster — a woman who's never married
cawing — making the sound of a crow
slewed — twisted sideways
puce — a deep red or purple colour
fluent — flowing or speaking smoothly

Havisham

Key Poem

Miss Havisham was a character in *Great Expectations* by Charles Dickens. She was <u>stood up</u> on her wedding day and ended up a bit mad, staying in her wedding dress for years with the rotting cake in her room. In this poem, Duffy describes her feelings. It's a tad bitter and twisted, this one...

You've Got to Know What Happens in the Poem

<u>Lines 1-4</u>	Havisham's dead <u>angry</u>. She wants to <u>kill</u> the man who stood her up.
<u>Lines 5-9</u>	She describes the weird things she does — like staying in bed all day <u>screaming</u>, and always wearing her old, manky <u>wedding dress</u>.
<u>Lines 9-12</u>	She says she sometimes dreams there's a man <u>in bed with her</u>, then wakes up abruptly.
<u>Lines 12-16</u>	She tells us that she stabbed the cake, but really wants to <u>stab a man</u>.

Learn About the Three Types of Language

1) <u>VIOLENT LANGUAGE</u> — Havisham's hell-bent on <u>revenge</u>. She wants to <u>take out her anger</u> on a man — but settles for <u>stabbing</u> the wedding-cake instead.

2) <u>REFLECTIVE LANGUAGE</u> — There are signs that she <u>hasn't always</u> been a nutter. At times she <u>reflects</u> on how she's become like she is, and we see a more <u>sensitive</u> side to her.

3) <u>WEDDING-RELATED LANGUAGE</u> — There are plenty of <u>images of weddings</u> — but instead of being signs of love and happiness, they stand for Havisham's <u>bitterness</u> and <u>violent streak</u>.

Remember the Feelings and Attitudes in the Poem

"I could murder a slice of cake..."

1) <u>ANGER</u> — Havisham is really really really really <u>angry</u> — at the man who stood her up, and also at men in general.

2) <u>BITTERNESS</u> — She's very very very <u>bitter</u> about it too. She wants to get <u>revenge</u>.

3) <u>SADNESS</u> — She's also <u>unhappy</u> — she uses her violent feelings to cover up the fact that she's actually very <u>upset</u> and <u>vulnerable</u> because she was dumped on her big day.

> Havisham is totally <u>obsessed</u> by what's happened to her. She can't think about anything else, even though it happened years ago.

Think About Your Feelings and Attitudes to the Poem

1) Pick 2 words or phrases that <u>stand out to you</u>. If none stand out, just pick 2 <u>unusual words or phrases</u>.

2) Write these 2 words or phrases down. Then write about how they <u>make you feel</u>. If they don't make you feel anything, don't worry — just <u>make something up</u>, as long as it's not too stupid.

> **EXAMPLE** When Havisham describes herself "trembling if I open the wardrobe", I feel sorry for her. She's so scared of what she has become that she can't even bear to look at herself in the mirror.

Themes — mood, strong emotions and the first person...

Compare 'Havisham' with other poems about the same themes: <u>mood</u> ('Tichborne's Elegy p.14-15), <u>strong emotions</u> ('Those bastards in their mansions' p.62-63 and 'The Affliction of Margaret' p.10-11) and use of the <u>first person</u> ('Kid' p.60-61 and 'Ulysses' p.26-27).

Section Two — Carol Ann Duffy

Elvis's Twin Sister

Elvis's Twin Sister

Are you lonesome tonight? Do you miss me tonight?

Elvis is alive and she's female: Madonna

> She leads a simple, peaceful life.

> This greeting reveals her background. She's from the southern USA, like her brother.

> Sounds like a typical religious activity, but the next line makes the link with Elvis.

In the convent, y'all,
I tend the gardens,
watch things grow,
pray for the immortal soul
5   of rock 'n' roll.

> This name combines both aspects of her personality.

> Funny image of Elvis's sexy movements in a convent.

They call me
Sister Presley here.
The Reverend Mother
digs the way I move my hips
10   just like my brother.

> Peaceful religious singing contrasts with Elvis's rock 'n' roll.

> A hymn sung at Easter — religion is central to her life.

Gregorian chant
drifts out across the herbs
Pascha nostrum immolatus est ...
I wear a simple habit,
15   darkish hues,

> She has the usual basic clothes and possessions of a nun. They're functional, not fashionable.

> A similarity with her brother.

a wimple with a novice-sewn
lace band, a rosary,
a chain of keys,
a pair of good and sturdy
20   blue suede shoes.

> She loves the convent like Elvis loved his home.

> Another famous Elvis characteristic.

I think of it
as Graceland here,
a land of grace.
It puts my trademark slow lopsided smile
25   back on my face.

> Slang way of saying "lord" links the religious and rock 'n' roll parts of her background.

> This refers to the rumours that "Elvis lives".

> Places from Elvis songs. Heartbreak and loneliness are things of the past now.

Lawdy.
I'm alive and well.
Long time since I walked
down Lonely Street
30   towards Heartbreak Hotel.

POEM DICTIONARY
convent — a place where nuns live
habit — a dress worn by a nun
wimple — a piece of cloth that a nun wears around her head
Graceland — the home of Elvis Presley
Gregorian chant — a religious style of singing in harmony
hues — shades, colours
rosary — religious beads
Heartbreak Hotel — name of an Elvis Presley song

Section Two — Carol Ann Duffy

Elvis's Twin Sister

The poet imagines that Elvis Presley has a twin sister who's living as a nun (in real life Elvis didn't have a sister). If only we could persuade Gareth Gates to be a monk...

You've Got to Know What Happens in the Poem

Lines 1-10	Elvis's imaginary sister talks about her simple, peaceful life as a nun. She hints at her similarity in appearance to Elvis (lines 8-10).
Lines 11-20	She describes the religious singing that rings out around the convent. She says she wears simple, practical clothes.
Lines 21-30	She's really happy at the convent — she's left her sadness behind.

Learn About the Three Types of Language

1) ELVIS REFERENCES — Lots of famous aspects of Elvis's life (like his songs, looks and clothes) are used to strengthen the idea that the nun is just like him — she's just chosen a different way of life.

2) RELIGIOUS LANGUAGE — The simple clothes and religious lifestyle of the nuns contrast with the fancy life that Elvis led.

3) HUMOUR — The idea of a nun looking and acting like Elvis is pretty funny when you think about it. It adds a light-hearted touch to the poem.

Remember the Feelings and Attitudes in the Poem

1) CONTENTMENT — Elvis's sister is happy living her simple life.

2) HUMOUR — There's a light-hearted feel to the poem — the idea of a nun looking and acting like Elvis is quite funny.

Think About Your Feelings and Attitudes to the Poem

1) Pick 2 words or phrases that stand out to you. If none stand out, just pick 2 unusual words or phrases.

2) Write these 2 words or phrases down. Then write about how they make you feel. If they don't make you feel anything, don't worry — just make something up, as long as it's not too stupid.

> **EXAMPLE** When Elvis's sister says "The Reverend Mother / digs the way I move my hips", it makes me laugh. The idea of a nun moving like Elvis is funny, but by using the word "digs", Duffy makes it sound like the Reverend Mother is attracted to Elvis's sister just like a fan might be attracted to Elvis. This is funny because nuns are supposed to be well-behaved and more serious than that.

Themes — characters, the first person and imagery...

Compare 'Elvis's Twin Sister' with other poems about the same themes: strong characters ('Salome' p.42-43 and 'My Last Duchess' p.22-23), use of the first person ('My father thought it bloody queer' p.54-55 and 'The Song of the Old Mother' p.8-9) and imagery ('Kid' p.60-61 and 'Sonnet' p.34-35).

Anne Hathaway

Anne Hathaway

'Item I gyve unto my wife my second best bed ...'

(from Shakespeare's will)

This is how she remembers it, rather than the "second best bed".

She feels that he took her to romantic, exciting places — it's like being in a fairytale.

Shows their love was rare and magical.

Their life was a fantasy.

Other people speak in boring prose — not beautiful poetry like Shakespeare.

She felt safe and secure with him.

Her experiences with Shakespeare were everything to her.

She sees their love as a hidden treasure.

Their bodies fit together, like a rhyming couplet.

He gave her life and movement.

Sounds ordinary and dull, contrasting with what happened in Anne's bed.

Alliteration emphasises how alive she felt when she was with him.

His resting place is inside her head.

The bed we loved in was a spinning world
of forests, castles, torchlight, clifftops, seas
where he would dive for pearls. My lover's words
were shooting stars which fell to earth as kisses
5 on these lips; my body now a softer rhyme
to his, now echo, assonance; his touch
a verb dancing in the centre of a noun.
Some nights, I dreamed he'd written me, the bed
a page beneath his writer's hands. Romance
10 and drama played by touch, by scent, by taste.
In the other bed, the best, our guests dozed on,
dribbling their prose. My living laughing love –
I hold him in the casket of my widow's head
as he held me upon that next best bed.

POEM DICTIONARY
Anne Hathaway — Shakespeare's wife
prose — normal writing or speech (not poetry)
casket — a small box for valuables, sometimes used to mean a coffin

Anne Hathaway

In this poem, Duffy writes as <u>Shakespeare's wife</u>, Anne Hathaway. Like many love poems written by Shakespeare himself, it's a <u>sonnet</u> — a kind of poem with 14 lines. The poem's about what went on in the "second best bed" that Shakespeare left Anne in his will.

You've Got to Know What Happens in the Poem

<u>Lines 1-7</u>   Anne describes her memories of the <u>bed</u>. It reminded her of fond memories of her <u>passionate love</u> with Shakespeare. She compares his love to the words in his <u>poems</u>.

<u>Lines 8-10</u>   She seems to see their love as one of Shakespeare's <u>plays</u>.

<u>Lines 11-14</u>   Their guests had the better bed <u>but</u> Anne and Shakespeare had the better love. She says she'll always <u>remember</u> the love between them in that bed (lines 13-14).

Learn About the Two Types of Language

1) <u>ROMANTIC LANGUAGE</u> — There are some quite <u>traditional</u> romantic metaphors, especially in the first few lines. This shows how <u>precious</u> and <u>amazing</u> Anne's time with Shakespeare was.

2) <u>REFERENCES TO PLAYS AND POEMS</u> — She compares the way Shakespeare loved her to his <u>writing methods</u>. Poetic techniques like <u>rhyming</u> and <u>assonance</u> are mentioned (see the <u>glossary</u> if you don't know what these words mean). Their love was so intense that it seemed <u>poetic</u> — Anne felt like she was in a <u>play</u>, rather than the real world.

Remember the Feelings and Attitudes in the Poem

1) <u>FONDNESS</u> — Anne has <u>fond memories</u> of Shakespeare.

2) <u>EXCITEMENT</u> — She's <u>excited</u> just remembering what it was like being with him.

3) <u>FANTASY</u> — She feels like they were in their <u>own world</u>, where everything seemed magical, like a <u>fantasy</u>.

Think About Your Feelings and Attitudes to the Poem

1) Pick 2 words or phrases that <u>stand out to you</u>. If none stand out, just pick 2 <u>unusual words or phrases</u>.

2) Write these 2 words or phrases down. Then write about how they <u>make you feel</u>. If they don't make you feel anything, don't worry — just <u>make something up</u>, as long as it's not too stupid.

> **EXAMPLE** I think it's really beautiful when Anne says "My lover's words / were shooting stars". It reminds me of how excited I feel when I read my boyfriend's love letters to me.

Themes — love, memory and closing couplets...

Compare 'Anne Hathaway' with other poems about the same themes: <u>love</u> ('Mother, any distance...' p.52-53 and 'On my first Sonne' p.6-7), <u>memory</u> ('We Remember Your Childhood Well' p.46-47 and 'My Last Duchess' p.22-23) and a <u>closing couplet</u> ('Sonnet 130' p.20-21).

Salome

Salome

She's only slightly regretful — which is shocking when we realise what she's actually done.

Sounds like she's having a light-hearted chat with a friend.

The coldness hints at what we find out later — he's dead.

She complains about minor problems like being hungover, but doesn't seem bothered about the man she's killed.

Without knowing who he is, she assumes he's violent.

She makes her connection to Salome clear — we expect the worst now.

Black humour — she doesn't tell us that there isn't a body attached to the head.

At first we think this means his hair is thick or tangled — but it could actually be matted with blood.

Sounds natural and normal here — but the colouring is really from blood stains.

Rhyming, here and in other verses, makes her sound in control — she didn't do it by accident.

Common, everyday sayings suggest she's a normal person with normal problems.

Light-hearted expression.

Christian image of innocence — now he's the victim.

An evil look before she reveals the truth.

Sarcastically pretends to be bothered — she doesn't seem to really care about what she's done.

The poem finishes in a shocking way. But even here, her tone is calm.

I'd done it before
(and doubtless I'll do it again,
sooner or later)
woke up with a head on the pillow beside me – whose? –
5 what did it matter?
Good-looking, of course, dark hair, rather matted;
the reddish beard several shades lighter;
with very deep lines around the eyes,
from pain, I'd guess, maybe laughter;
10 and a beautiful crimson mouth that obviously knew
how to flatter ...
which I kissed ...
Colder than pewter.
Strange. What was his name? Peter?

15 Simon? Andrew? John? I knew I'd feel better
for tea, dry toast, no butter,
so rang for the maid.
And, indeed, her innocent clatter
of cups and plates,
20 her clearing of clutter,
her regional patter,
were just what needed –
hungover and wrecked as I was from a night on the batter.

Never again!
25 I needed to clean up my act,
get fitter,
cut out the booze and the fags and the sex.
Yes. And as for the latter,
it was time to turf out the blighter,
30 the beater or biter,
who'd come like a lamb to the slaughter
to Salome's bed.

In the mirror, I saw my eyes glitter.
I flung back the sticky red sheets,
35 and there, like I said – and ain't life a bitch –
was his head on a platter.

POEM DICTIONARY
Salome — Biblical woman who tricked Herod into giving her the head of John the Baptist on a plate
crimson — a deep red colour
pewter — a kind of metal, made up mainly of tin
patter — speech
platter — a large dish for food

Salome

This poem's pretty grim. The woman in the poem wakes up after a <u>one-night stand</u>, after getting drunk the night before. She regrets it and says she needs to stop doing this sort of thing. Then it turns out she's <u>cut the bloke's head off</u>. Nice.

You've Got to Know What Happens in the Poem

<u>Lines 1-14</u>	The character in the poem wakes up with a <u>man's head</u> on the pillow next to her. She <u>can't remember</u> who he is.
<u>Lines 15-23</u>	She calls for her <u>maid</u>, who enters making loads of <u>noise</u>.
<u>Lines 24-32</u>	She says she needs to <u>cut out</u> her unhealthy habits and <u>get rid</u> of the man in her bed.
<u>Lines 33-36</u>	She pulls the sheets back, and we realise there's nothing there but his <u>severed head</u>.

Learn About the Three Types of Language

1) <u>DOUBLE MEANINGS</u> — Some of the language in the poem can be read in a <u>different way</u> after finding out that she's actually <u>killed</u> the man, rather than just sleeping with him. There's some <u>black humour</u> in the double meanings — they're both <u>horrible and funny</u> at the same time.

2) <u>CASUAL LANGUAGE</u> — The woman describes the incident as if it's just a <u>normal event</u>. Her <u>casual tone</u> is really <u>shocking</u> when we realise the full horror of what she's done.

3) <u>BIBLICAL REFERENCES</u> — The poem is set in the <u>modern day</u>, but there are references to <u>religious stories</u> which connect what happens to the story of <u>Salome</u> in the bible.

Remember the Feelings and Attitudes in the Poem

"More blood, ma'am?"

1) <u>CASUALNESS</u> — At first, the woman seems a bit <u>regretful</u> — but we soon start to realise that she's <u>not all that bothered</u>.

2) <u>NASTINESS</u> — We see her <u>evil</u> side at the end of the poem.

3) <u>PRIDE</u> — She even seems quite <u>proud</u> of killing the man — she seems to <u>enjoy</u> letting us think she's only slept with him, before dramatically revealing the truth at the end of the poem.

Think About Your Feelings and Attitudes to the Poem

1) Pick 2 words or phrases that <u>stand out to you</u>. If none stand out, just pick 2 <u>unusual words or phrases</u>.

2) Write these 2 words or phrases down. Then write about how they <u>make you feel</u>. If they don't make you feel anything, don't worry — just <u>make something up</u>, as long as it's not too stupid.

> **EXAMPLE** The line "I flung back the sticky red sheets" makes me feel sick. I find it disgusting that she could be lying there in a bed drenched in blood, talking calmly about chopping off a man's head.

Themes — evil, irony and characters...

Compare 'Salome' with other poems about the same themes: <u>evil</u> ('Hitcher' p.66-67 and 'My Last Duchess' p.22-23), <u>irony</u> ('Tichborne's Elegy' p.14-15 and 'The Man He Killed' p.16-17), and <u>character</u> ('Havisham' p.36-37 and 'The Laboratory' p.30-31).

Before You Were Mine

The first 3 verses each start with a reminder of the distance in time between the poet's birth and her mum's youth and fun.

The poet talks directly to her mum.

Her mother's life was fun before she was born.

Compares her mother with Marilyn Monroe — she was glamorous and desirable.

Before You Were Mine

I'm ten years away from the corner you laugh on
with your pals, Maggie McGeeney and Jean Duff.
The three of you bend from the waist, holding
each other, or your knees, and shriek at the pavement.
5   Your polka-dot dress blows round your legs. Marilyn.

I'm not here yet. The thought of me doesn't occur
in the ballroom with the thousand eyes, the fizzy, movie tomorrows
the right walk home could bring. I knew you would dance
like that. Before you were mine, your Ma stands at the close
10   with a hiding for the late one. You reckon it's worth it.

The decade ahead of my loud, possessive yell was the best one, eh?
I remember my hands in those high-heeled red shoes, relics,
and now your ghost clatters toward me over George Square
till I see you, clear as scent, under the tree,
15   with its lights, and whose small bites on your neck, sweetheart?

Cha cha cha! You'd teach me the steps on the way home from Mass,
stamping stars from the wrong pavement. Even then
I wanted the bold girl winking in Portobello, somewhere
in Scotland, before I was born. That glamorous love lasts
20   where you sparkle and waltz and laugh before you were mine.

Her mum was the centre of attention and had exciting opportunities.

She used to belong to herself, not someone else.

Her mum was wasn't scared of the consequences of enjoying herself.

The poet was a demanding baby.

The glamour is a thing of the past, and won't return.

Sounds like something a parent would say to their child, but here it's the other way around.

Alliteration

Emphasises that the poet's birth was the turning point in her mum's life.

She was bright, energetic and fun-loving.

POEM DICTIONARY
Marilyn — Marilyn Monroe (a famous film star from the 1950s)
relics — old things from a past time
Cha cha cha — a Latin-American ballroom dance

Section Two — Carol Ann Duffy

Before You Were Mine

The poet talks to her mother about the ten years before her birth. She imagines her mum leading a fun-filled, _carefree_ life. But that all changed when she became a mother and her _freedom_ went. She wants her mum to be that happy and fun-loving girl again, but realises she only exists in the past.

You've Got to Know What Happens in the Poem

<u>Lines 1-5</u>	The poet describes her mum having fun with <u>friends</u>. She compares her with <u>Marilyn Monroe</u>.
<u>Lines 6-11</u>	Her mum stayed out late <u>dancing</u>, not put off by being <u>told off</u> by her own mother. The poet says that her mother was <u>happiest</u> during the 10 years before she was born.
<u>Lines 12-15</u>	The poet remembers <u>glimpses</u> of her mum's fun-loving past from when she was a <u>child</u>.
<u>Lines 16-20</u>	She remembers her mum teaching her to <u>dance</u>. She wanted her to be like this more often, but realises that she was only really fun-loving and glamorous <u>before</u> she was born.

Learn About the Three Types of Language

1) <u>EXCITING LANGUAGE</u> — There are loads of words and phrases which describe how <u>exciting</u>, <u>fun</u> and <u>glamorous</u> the poet's mum's life was before the poet was born.

2) <u>POSSESSIVE LANGUAGE</u> — It seems that when the poet was born, she <u>took control</u> of her mum, and her mum couldn't be <u>free</u> any more. The idea of <u>breaking free</u> from your parents is turned on its head, with the child stopping the parent from having fun.

3) <u>LANGUAGE ABOUT TIME</u> — There's a very clear <u>division</u> between the time <u>before</u> the poet was born and the time <u>after</u> she was born, when her mum's glamorous life came to an <u>abrupt end</u>.

Remember the Feelings and Attitudes in the Poem

Not to be confused with Marilyn Manson.

1) <u>ADMIRATION</u> — The poet <u>admires</u> her mum's headstrong, rebellious approach to life.

2) <u>NOSTALGIA</u> — She wishes her mum was <u>still fun-loving</u> and carefree.

3) <u>SELF-CRITICISM</u> — The poet seems to <u>criticise</u> herself for taking away her mum's freedom (line 11).

Think About Your Feelings and Attitudes to the Poem

1) Pick 2 words or phrases that <u>stand out to you</u>. If none stand out, just pick 2 <u>unusual words or phrases</u>.

2) Write these 2 words or phrases down. Then write about how they <u>make you feel</u>. If they don't make you feel anything, don't worry — just <u>make something up</u>, as long as it's not too stupid.

> **EXAMPLE** When the poet says "I wanted the bold girl winking in Portobello", it makes me sad. She seems to admire the happy, rebellious side of her mother more than the responsible parent side, but the poet knows that she is the very reason for the change in her mother's lifestyle.

Themes — parent/child, getting older, imagery...

Compare 'Before You Were Mine' with other poems about the same themes: <u>parent/child relationships</u> ('My father thought it bloody queer' p.54-55), <u>getting older</u> ('Mother, any distance' p.52-53) and <u>imagery</u> ('Homecoming' p.56-57 and 'Kid' p.60-61).

We Remember Your Childhood Well

We know they wouldn't say this if there hadn't been an accusation.

The memories are very negative.

This refers to the child murders on the Lancashire moors in the 1960s.

We Remember Your Childhood Well

Nobody hurt you. Nobody turned off the light and argued
with somebody else all night. The bad man on the moors
was only a movie you saw. Nobody locked the door.

Your questions were answered fully. No. That didn't occur.
5 You couldn't sing anyway, cared less. The moment's a blur, a *Film Fun*
laughing itself to death in the coal fire. Anyone's guess.

They make it as vague as possible, to try to confuse the person and cover up the truth.

They say that it was the child's choice.

Nobody forced you. You wanted to go that day. Begged. You chose
the dress. Here are the pictures, look at you. Look at us all,
smiling and waving, younger. The whole thing is inside your head.

They use images of happiness to cover up the painful truth.

At least they're honest here — they were in charge.

10 What you recall are impressions; we have the facts. We called the tune.
The secret police of your childhood were older and wiser than you, bigger
than you. Call back the sound of their voices. Boom. Boom. Boom.

Sounds sinister and controlling.

The voices were loud and angry.

Nobody sent you away. That was an extra holiday, with people
you seemed to like. They were firm, there was nothing to fear.
15 There was none but yourself to blame if it ended in tears.

They even tell the person what his/her own feelings and opinions were.

They're denying it more strongly.

What does it matter now? No, no, nobody left the skidmarks of sin
on your soul and laid you wide open for Hell. You were loved.
Always. We did what was best. We remember your childhood well.

Suggests the pain of the person's childhood still affects him/her now.

They say that it was the child's fault.

They insist that they remember what happened better than the person whose childhood is being discussed.

POEM DICTIONARY
occur — happen
Film Fun — a magazine about films

We Remember Your Childhood Well

In this poem, the people speaking <u>deny</u> that anything <u>bad</u> happened in someone's childhood (possibly their son or daughter). The child seems to have claimed he or she was abused, but we <u>never hear</u> that side of the story, so we can only guess what happened from what the people denying it say.

You've Got to Know *What Happens in the Poem*

<u>Lines 1-3</u>	The people speaking deny the claim that the person they're speaking to was <u>abused</u> as a child.
<u>Lines 4-6</u>	There are more <u>denials</u>. They say the child was never really bothered about <u>singing</u>.
<u>Lines 7-9</u>	They deny <u>forcing</u> the child to go somewhere. They say the child <u>wanted</u> to go, and enjoyed it.
<u>Lines 10-12</u>	Aggressively, they say that they're the only ones who can remember <u>what really happened</u>.
<u>Lines 13-18</u>	They again <u>deny</u> sending the child away. They tell the child that it was his/her <u>own fault</u> if anything bad happened. They say they treated the child <u>well</u>.

Learn About the *Three Types of Language*

1) <u>DENIAL</u> — We don't hear the accusations, but the denials give us <u>clues</u> as to what they are. There's a <u>defensive</u> tone right from the start — we can tell the people speaking are <u>covering something up</u>.

2) <u>AGGRESSION</u> — The tone becomes more <u>threatening</u> as the poem goes on. The people speaking find it more and more difficult to pretend to be pleasant, and in the end resort to <u>threats</u> and <u>guilt trips</u>.

3) <u>PAIN and FEAR</u> — The childhood memories are <u>confused</u> and <u>scary</u>. The fact that we <u>don't find out</u> exactly what happened increases the sense of fear in the poem. Past events seem to have caused <u>lasting pain</u> to the person, even after they grew up.

Remember the *Feelings and Attitudes in the Poem*

1) <u>CRUELTY</u> — There's a <u>cruel</u>, <u>sinister</u> feel to the poem.

2) <u>SUSPICION</u> — We suspect that <u>bad things</u> happened to the child, but the people speaking are trying to <u>cover up</u> the truth.

3) <u>GUILT</u> — They even try to make the <u>victim</u> feel that what happened was his/her <u>fault</u>.

4) <u>PAIN</u> — There's a real sense of <u>pain</u> and <u>sadness</u> — it seems that the person's life has been <u>ruined</u> by the events in his/her childhood (lines 16-17).

Think About Your *Feelings and Attitudes to the Poem*

1) Pick 2 words or phrases that <u>stand out to you</u>. If none stand out, just pick 2 <u>unusual words or phrases</u>.

2) Write these 2 words or phrases down. Then write about how they <u>make you feel</u>. If they don't make you feel anything, don't worry — just <u>make something up</u>, as long as it's not too stupid.

> **EXAMPLE** When the people in the poem say "There was none but yourself to blame if it ended in tears", I feel angry. Trying to make someone feel guilty for something that happened when they were a child is a very cruel thing to do.

Themes — *mood, attitudes towards others, memory...*

Compare 'We Remember Your Childhood Well' to other poems about the same themes: <u>mood</u> ('Hitcher' p.66-67, 'The Little Boy Lost' and 'The Little Boy Found' p.12-13), <u>attitudes towards other people</u> ('My Last Duchess' p.22-23) and <u>memory</u> ('Homecoming' p.56-57).

Section Two — Carol Ann Duffy

Key Poem

Education for Leisure

Education for Leisure

The character wants attention.

Wants to be grand and powerful.

Not a very impressive thing to do.

Very arrogant. There's nothing to back this claim up.

Blames others for his/her own failures.

Pathetic but funny attempt at being powerful.

Sounds disappointed.

Excitement contrasts with line 4.

Matter-of-fact tone is chilling.

Alliteration

The character felt left out — he/she couldn't understand it.

Another boast — but it seems he/she hasn't achieved anything yet.

This ambitious claim contrasts with what he/she actually does.

Scaring the pets is a pretty poor attempt at being powerful.

Thinks he/she deserves to be recognised.

Suggests the character is famous and popular, but we know this isn't true.

Purposeful, violent tone.

Now the character threatens the reader.

Today I am going to kill something. Anything.
I have had enough of being ignored and today
I am going to play God. It is an ordinary day,
a sort of grey with boredom stirring in the streets.

5 I squash a fly against the window with my thumb.
We did that at school. Shakespeare. It was in
another language and now the fly is in another language.
I breathe out talent on the glass to write my name.

I am a genius. I could be anything at all, with half
10 the chance. But today I am going to change the world.
Something's world. The cat avoids me. The cat
knows I am a genius, and has hidden itself.

I pour the goldfish down the bog. I pull the chain.
I see that it is good. The budgie is panicking.
15 Once a fortnight, I walk the two miles into town
for signing on. They don't appreciate my autograph.

There is nothing left to kill. I dial the radio
and tell the man he's talking to a superstar.
He cuts me off. I get our bread-knife and go out.
20 The pavements glitter suddenly. I touch your arm.

POEM DICTIONARY
signing on — registering for unemployment benefit

Section Two — Carol Ann Duffy

Education for Leisure

The person in this poem is a bit disturbed. Fed up of feeling bored and ignored, he/she goes on a <u>killing spree</u>, starting with animals. Then he/she goes outside with a <u>knife</u>, presumably to kill people, although we don't find out exactly what happens then. I just read a book when I'm bored...

You've Got to Know What Happens in the Poem

<u>Lines 1-4</u>   The person in the poem is <u>bored</u> and <u>restless</u>, so he/she decides to <u>kill something</u>.

<u>Lines 5-7</u>   The character kills a <u>fly</u>, which makes him/her think of how he/she felt <u>excluded</u> at school.

<u>Lines 8-14</u>   The character says he/she's a <u>genius</u> and is <u>determined</u> to prove it.
                 He/she enjoys the <u>power</u> of <u>killing the pets</u> in the house.

<u>Lines 15-20</u> The character is <u>annoyed</u> that no-one recognises or respects him/her.
                 He/she gets a <u>knife</u> and goes outside.

Learn About the Three Types of Language

1) <u>VIOLENT LANGUAGE</u> — The person in the poem kills <u>everything he/she can find</u> in the house, then goes outside to continue the <u>killing spree</u>. The really shocking thing about the violence is the character's <u>calm tone</u> — as if he/she's describing <u>normal</u> and <u>reasonable</u> behaviour.

2) <u>BOASTFUL LANGUAGE</u> — The character seems really <u>arrogant</u>. Loads of the sentences begin with "I", showing how <u>self-obsessed</u> he/she is.

3) <u>LANGUAGE OF REJECTION</u> — The character feels <u>rejected</u> and <u>left out</u>. He/she wants to be well-known instead of ignored, and the mindless violence is a way of trying to be <u>recognised</u>.

Remember the Feelings and Attitudes in the Poem

"Uh-oh..."

1) <u>RESENTMENT</u> — The character <u>resents</u> the way people <u>ignore</u> him/her.

2) <u>GRIM DETERMINATION</u> — The character's <u>determined</u> to make his/her mark on the world, by showing how <u>powerful</u> he/she is.

3) <u>CALMNESS</u> — This person is very <u>laid back</u> about all the killing.

4) <u>ENJOYMENT</u> — The character <u>enjoys</u> the sense of power he/she gets from killing.

> Clearly this individual has <u>lost the plot</u> — he or she thinks killing the fish is a sign of genius, and seems ready to kill anyone just to get attention.

Think About Your Feelings and Attitudes to the Poem

1) Pick 2 words or phrases that <u>stand out to you</u>. If none stand out, just pick 2 <u>unusual words or phrases</u>.

2) Write these 2 words or phrases down. Then write about how they <u>make you feel</u>. If they don't make you feel anything, don't worry — just <u>make something up</u>, as long as it's not too stupid.

> **EXAMPLE** When the person in the poem says "I touch your arm", it sends a chill down my spine. At this point it seems that, now he/she has run out of animals to kill, he will kill anyone he finds, starting with the reader.

Themes — danger, death, the first person...

Compare 'Education for Leisure' with other poems about the same themes: <u>danger</u> ('Stealing' p.50-51 and 'Those bastards in their mansions' p.62-63), <u>death</u> ('Hitcher' p.66-67 and 'The Man He Killed' p.16-17) and use of the first person ('Kid' p.60-61 and 'The Laboratory' p.30-31).

Section Two — Carol Ann Duffy

Stealing

Stealing

Alliteration

The most unusual thing I ever stole? A snowman.
Midnight. He looked magnificent; a tall, white mute
beneath the winter moon. I wanted him, a mate
with a mind as cold as the slice of ice
5   within my own brain. I started with the head.

The snowman can't communicate, like the character in the poem.

Rhyming makes these 2 words seem connected.

The split rhyme emphasises the cold feeling.

Better off dead than giving in, not taking
what you want. He weighed a ton; his torso,
frozen stiff, hugged to my chest, a fierce chill
piercing my gut. Part of the thrill was knowing
10   that children would cry in the morning. Life's tough.

Seems to be boasting here.

Offhand comment — doesn't care about the effects on other people.

This metaphor suggests the narrator spoils things, and also that he/she feels dead like a ghost.

Sometimes I steal things I don't need. I joy-ride cars
to nowhere, break into houses just to have a look.
I'm a mucky ghost, leave a mess, maybe pinch a camera.
I watch my gloved hand twisting the doorknob.
15   A stranger's bedroom. Mirrors. I sigh like this – *Aah.*

Use of slang shows the character's casual approach to theft.

Sounds both threatening and sad — the character's life is lonely and unreal.

It took some time. Reassembled in the yard,
he didn't look the same. I took a run
and booted him. Again. Again. My breath ripped out
in rags. It seems daft now. Then I was standing
20   alone amongst lumps of snow, sick of the world.

The character's actions are damaging his/her own body.

Realises how pointless and silly it sounds.

Boredom. Mostly I'm so bored I could eat myself.
One time, I stole a guitar and thought I might
learn to play. I nicked a bust of Shakespeare once,
flogged it, but the snowman was strangest.
25   You don't understand a word I'm saying, do you?

Self-destructive and pointless.

More slang words.

Realises that he/she isn't making any sense.

POEM DICTIONARY
torso — middle part of a body
pinch — steal
reassembled — put back together
bust — a statue of someone's head and shoulders

Stealing

The rather strange character in the poem remembers <u>stealing a snowman</u>. Then he/she describes stealing lots of other things because he/she was <u>bored</u>. The dirty tea-leaf.

You've Got to Know What Happens in the Poem

<u>Lines 1-10</u>	The character in the poem remembers stealing a <u>snowman</u> at night, bit by bit. This seems to have been for <u>company</u>, and also to make the children who made it cry.
<u>Lines 11-15</u>	The character describes stealing cars, cameras and other things — and getting a <u>thrill</u> from it.
<u>Lines 16-20</u>	The character couldn't put the snowman back together properly — so he/she <u>destroyed</u> it.
<u>Lines 21-25</u>	The character says he/she steals because of <u>boredom</u>, but can't seem to explain it properly.

Learn About the Three Types of Language

1) <u>SIMILES</u> and <u>METAPHORS</u> — There's also some quite <u>descriptive</u> language, which <u>contrasts</u> with the down-to-earth tone in most of the poem. It's as if his/her <u>real feelings</u> are struggling to come out.

2) <u>SOUND EFFECTS</u> — The irregular <u>rhymes</u>, sometimes between words on the same line, and <u>alliteration</u> draw the reader's attention to certain combinations of words.

3) <u>CONVERSATIONAL LANGUAGE</u> — It feels like the character is <u>talking directly</u> to us. His/her chatty tone of voice shows how <u>casual</u> he/she is about stealing.

Remember the Feelings and Attitudes in the Poem

1) <u>ENTHUSIASM</u> — At the start of the poem, the thief is <u>enthusiastic</u> about explaining why he/she steals things.

2) <u>BOREDOM</u> — By the end, <u>loneliness</u> and <u>boredom</u> take over.

3) <u>FRUSTRATION</u> — He/she is <u>frustrated</u> and <u>angry</u> when destroying the snowman.

4) <u>POINTLESSNESS</u> — At the end, he/she feels the whole attempt to explain it is <u>a waste of time</u>.

Think About Your Feelings and Attitudes to the Poem

1) Pick 2 words or phrases that <u>stand out to you</u>. If none stand out, just pick 2 <u>unusual words or phrases</u>.

2) Write these 2 words or phrases down. Then write about how they <u>make you feel</u>. If they don't make you feel anything, don't worry — just <u>make something up</u>, as long as it's not too stupid.

> **EXAMPLE** The statement "better off dead than giving in, not taking / what you want" makes me angry with the person in the poem. He/she is trying to come across as bold and decisive, but this sentence really shows how selfish the character is, not thinking about anyone but him/herself.

Themes — attitudes towards others, danger, language...

Compare 'Stealing' with other poems about the same themes: <u>attitudes towards others</u> ('November' p.58-59 and 'Hitcher' p.66-67), <u>danger</u> ('Education for Leisure' p.48-49 and 'Those bastards in their mansions' p.62-63) and <u>language effects</u> ('The Laboratory' p.30-31 and 'Kid' p.60-61).

Mother, any distance

Simon Armitage was born in 1963 in Huddersfield, West Yorkshire. As well as poetry, he's also written four stage plays, and writes for TV, film and radio. He studied at Leeds University and he now teaches at Manchester Metropolitan University.

from **Book of Matches**

> He addresses her directly. It's like a personal message to her.

Mother, any distance greater than a single span
requires a second pair of hands.
You come to help me measure windows, pelmets, doors,
the acres of the walls, the prairies of the floors.

> Without his mother, even the walls and floors seem big and frightening.

> His mother is holding the start of the tape measure.

5   You at the zero-end, me with the spool of tape, recording
length, reporting metres, centimetres back to base, then leaving
up the stairs, the line still feeding out, unreeling
years between us. Anchor. Kite.

> He moves upwards and away from his mother.

> They have to let go of their shared history.

> His mother will keep him from getting carried away.

I space-walk through the empty bedrooms, climb
10   the ladder to the loft, to breaking point, where something
has to give;
two floors below your fingertips still pinch
the last one-hundredth of an inch ... I reach
towards a hatch that opens on an endless sky
15   to fall or fly.

> They have to break their ties at some point.

> She's now only a small part of his life.

> She won't let go completely.

> He doesn't know if he'll succeed or fail.

POEM DICTIONARY
span — the distance between two points (e.g. between two arms outstretched)
pelmets — boards or material above a window which hide the curtain rail
prairies — grassy plains

Mother, any distance

In this poem, the poet is <u>moving out</u> of his mum's house. But he still needs her to help measure things in his new house, and this becomes a metaphor for how he can always <u>turn to her</u> for support if he needs to. Like when his laundry needs doing, probably...

You've Got to Know What Happens in the Poem

<u>Lines 1-4</u>   The poet's <u>mother</u> comes to the house he's moving into, to help <u>measure walls</u> and other things.

<u>Lines 5-8</u>   She holds the <u>end</u> of the tape measure while he walks away to measure things. This makes him think about how she's always <u>looked after him</u> — but now she has to <u>let him go</u>.

<u>Lines 9-15</u>   The poet is <u>looking forward</u> to being independent, but he's also a bit <u>scared</u> by it. He doesn't know if he'll <u>succeed</u> without his mum or not, but she'll <u>always be there</u> for him if he needs her.

Learn About the Two Types of Language

1) <u>LANGUAGE ABOUT MEASUREMENT</u> — Measurements and distances are an <u>extended metaphor</u> in this poem. They stand for the poet's changing relationship with his <u>mother</u>. They were once <u>close</u>, but they are now becoming more <u>distant</u>.

2) <u>LANGUAGE ABOUT MOVEMENT</u> — Walking around his own house is like <u>exploring</u> a new world. He feels ready to "<u>fly</u>" away from his mum (lines 13-15), but she seems ready to <u>catch him</u> if he falls (lines 12-13).

Remember the Feelings and Attitudes in the Poem

1) <u>EXCITEMENT</u> — The poet is <u>excited</u> about being independent in his new life.

2) <u>FEAR</u> — He's also <u>worried</u> by the thought of being on his own.

3) <u>ACCEPTANCE</u> — He <u>accepts</u> that his mother will always be a part of his life.

4) <u>APPRECIATION</u> — He seems to <u>appreciate</u> the fact that he can turn to her if he needs her.

Think About Your Feelings and Attitudes to the Poem

1) Pick 2 words or phrases that <u>stand out to you</u>. If none stand out, just pick 2 <u>unusual words or phrases</u>.

2) Write these 2 words or phrases down. Then write about how they <u>make you feel</u>. If they don't make you feel anything, don't worry — just <u>make something up</u>, as long as it's not too stupid.

EXAMPLE When the poet says "I space-walk through the empty bedrooms", I feel both excited and nervous for him. This line shows that breaking free from his mother is a big adventure for him, but also that he is now on his own in the big wide world.

Themes — parent/child relationships, getting older, imagery

Compare 'Mother, any distance...' with other poems about the same themes: <u>parent/child relationships</u> ('The Affliction of Margaret' p.10-11 and 'Before You Were Mine' p.44-45), <u>getting older</u> ('Kid' p.60-61) and <u>imagery</u> ('Anne Hathaway' p.40-41 and 'I've made out a will' p.64-65).

Section Three — Simon Armitage

Key Poem — My father thought it bloody queer

from Book of Matches

My father thought it bloody queer,
the day I rolled home with a ring of silver in my ear
half hidden by a mop of hair. 'You've lost your head.
If that's how easily you're led
5 you should've had it through your nose instead.'

And even then I hadn't had the nerve to numb
the lobe with ice, then drive a needle through the skin,
then wear a safety-pin. It took a jeweller's gun
to pierce the flesh, and then a friend
10 to thread a sleeper in, and where it slept
the hole became a sore, became a wound, and wept.

At twenty-nine, it comes as no surprise to hear
my own voice breaking like a tear, released like water,
cried from way back in the spiral of the ear. *If I were you,*
15 *I'd take it out and leave it out next year.*

The word "queer" could mean "odd" — but it could also mean his dad thinks the earring looks gay.

His scruffy hair-do shows he's trying to be a rebel.

Could mean either "You've gone mad" or "I can't even see your head any more".

Bulls are led around by a nose-ring — his dad says he got the earring because his mates told him to get one.

Sounds violent and painful.

This shows that it bled, and also suggests it made him cry with the pain — not very rebellious.

He's just hurt himself for no reason.

Remembering his dad's reaction upsets him.

It's not really clear who he's talking to here. But by saying the same things as his dad, it seems the poet has come to see things the same way his dad did.

This description suggests his emotions being bottled up, then suddenly flooding out.

POEM DICTIONARY
lobe — ear lobe
sleeper — a stud to stop a piercing from closing up
sore — wound

My father thought it bloody queer

Key Poem

The poet describes a time when he was a teenager and got his <u>ear pierced</u>. His dad wasn't impressed, and his attempt to be a rebel seemed a bit <u>stupid</u>. Now he's grown up, he hears himself saying the same things his dad said. Now where's my pipe...

You've Got to Know What Happens in the Poem

Lines 1-5   The poet remembers coming home after getting his <u>ear pierced</u>.
His <u>dad</u> took the mickey out of him and said it was <u>stupid</u>.

Lines 6-11   The poet says that he <u>wasn't brave enough</u> to pierce his own ear, so he
got a <u>jeweller</u> to do it. Afterwards, his ear went all sore and <u>bled</u>. Awww...

Lines 12-15   Now the poet's <u>grown up</u>, his dad's comments still upset him.
He says the <u>same things</u> his dad used to say.

Learn About the Three Types of Language

1)   <u>DESCRIPTIVE LANGUAGE</u> — The poet's <u>scruffy appearance</u> when he comes home
with the earring shows that he's a <u>typical teenager</u>. This makes him seem conventional
— not <u>rebellious</u> as he thought at the time.

2)   <u>AMBIGUOUS LANGUAGE</u> — A lot of the words and phrases in this poem are <u>ambiguous</u> —
they look like they have <u>one meaning</u>, then when you read them again they mean <u>something else</u>.

3)   <u>PAINFUL LANGUAGE</u> — The poet describes two kinds of pain — <u>physical pain</u> from having his
ear pierced, and <u>emotional pain</u> when he remembers his dad's reaction and how stupid he felt.

Remember the Feelings and Attitudes in the Poem

"Father, I want to be a doctor."

1)   <u>AMUSEMENT</u> — The poet's descriptions of his <u>funny appearance</u>
suggest he's <u>amused</u> when he remembers the incident.

2)   <u>REGRET</u> — But he's <u>upset</u> and <u>regretful</u> when he remembers
how <u>stupid</u> he felt after his dad's comments about the earring.

3)   <u>AGREEMENT</u> — At the end of the poem, he seems to have come
round to his <u>dad's point of view</u> — he now says the same kind
of things to kids that his dad said to him.

Think About Your Feelings and Attitudes to the Poem

1)   Pick 2 words or phrases that <u>stand out to you</u>. If none stand out, just pick 2 <u>unusual words or phrases</u>.

2)   Write these 2 words or phrases down. Then write about how they <u>make you feel</u>. If they don't make
you feel anything, don't worry — just <u>make something up</u>, as long as it's not too stupid.

> **EXAMPLE** When the poet says "It took a jeweller's gun / to pierce the flesh",
> it makes me wince with pain. It sounds like a horrible and pointless thing to
> put yourself through, just to try and look cool.

Themes — parent/child relationships, getting older, memory

Compare 'My father thought it...' with other poems about the same themes: <u>parent/child relationships</u>
('On my first Sonne' p.6-7 and 'Before You Were Mine' p.44-45), <u>getting older</u> ('Kid' p.60-61 and
'Mother, any distance...' p.52-53) and <u>memory</u> ('We Remember Your Childhood Well' p.46-47).

Homecoming

This applies to the whole poem — the poet wants to make you think.

Homecoming

Think, two things on their own and both at once.
The first, that exercise in trust, where those in front
stand with their arms spread wide and free-fall
backwards, blind, and those behind take all the weight.

5   The second, one canary-yellow cotton jacket
on a cloakroom floor, uncoupled from its hook,
becoming scuffed and blackened underfoot. Back home
the very model of a model of a mother, yours, puts
two and two together, makes a proper fist of it
10   and points the finger. Temper, temper. Questions
in the house. You seeing red. Blue murder. Bed.

Then midnight when you slip the latch and sneak
no further than the call-box at the corner of the street;
I'm waiting by the phone, although it doesn't ring
15   because it's sixteen years or so before we'll meet.
Retrace that walk towards the garden gate; in silhouette
a father figure waits there, wants to set things straight.

These ribs are pleats or seams. These arms are sleeves.
These fingertips are buttons, or these hands can fold
20   into a clasp, or else these fingers make a zip
or buckle, you say which. Step backwards into it
and try the same canary-yellow cotton jacket, there,
like this, for size again. It still fits.

He's saying the mother's perfect, but this could be sarcastic.

Here, colours represent strong words and emotions.

Usually this would sound protective, but the darkness makes us uncertain.

You have to make your own interpretation here, like in the poem as a whole.

This suggests the trust exercise and the jacket are related in some way.

The jacket seems bright and colourful — unlike the darkness and uncertainty of most of the memories in the poem.

This usually means just to have a good go at doing something, but the following lines make it sound more violent.

This gives us a clue — it seems that the poet is talking to someone about something that happened before they met.

Mysterious image. You can't make out any features of this person.

This could be well-meaning or threatening.

We don't know if these are his arms and ribs, or those of the person he's talking to.

This reminds us of the trust exercise at the start.

This could mean that the person hasn't changed.

POEM DICTIONARY
uncoupled — unlinked
model — excellent example of
silhouette — a person or object cast in dark shadow so that you can only see their outline
seams — sewn join between two pieces of fabric

Homecoming

This is a pretty confusing poem because it's not very clear exactly what's happening. There are some hazy memories of people sneaking about and getting told off. A yellow jacket is described, which seems to be a metaphor for people changing over time.

You've Got to Know What Happens in the Poem

Lines 1-4   The poet describes an exercise where people <u>learn to trust</u> someone.

Lines 5-11   A <u>yellow jacket</u> lies on the floor getting <u>trampled on</u>. Then someone, probably a young woman, gets <u>told off</u> by her mum for doing something wrong.

Lines 12-17   The same person sneaks off again, this time to a <u>phone box</u>. A <u>dark figure</u> waits by a gate.

Lines 18-23   The different parts of the <u>yellow jacket</u> are described as if they're parts of someone's <u>body</u>. It seems that the person <u>hasn't changed</u> much, because the jacket <u>still fits</u>.

Learn About the Three Types of Language

1)   <u>AMBIGUOUS LANGUAGE</u> — Lots of the images and description in the poem are <u>ambiguous</u> — we're not sure <u>what they mean</u>. This is often deliberate — it's supposed to make us stop and <u>think</u> about what the poet means.

2)   <u>COLOUR</u> — Most of the images in the poem are <u>dark</u> and <u>shadowy</u>, strengthening the vague and <u>uncertain</u> nature of the poem. The bright yellow colour of the <u>jacket</u> stands out.

3)   <u>METAPHORICAL LANGUAGE</u> — The <u>yellow jacket</u> becomes a metaphor, possibly for <u>behaviour</u> or <u>personality</u>. The jacket <u>still fits</u>, so maybe the person the poet is talking to <u>hasn't changed</u> much.

Remember the Feelings and Attitudes in the Poem

"Err, hello, police? I'm being stalked by a poet..."

1)   <u>ANGER</u> — The mother (lines 8-10) is very <u>angry</u> with her child.

2)   <u>TENSION</u> — We don't know how the "father figure" is going to "set things straight" (line 17).

3)   <u>UNCERTAINTY</u> — The poet wants us to <u>make our own minds up</u> about what the jacket stands for. We have to <u>make the connections</u> between the different things he describes.

> Don't worry if you find this poem really <u>confusing</u>. You don't have to completely understand it — as long as you can make some interesting points about it.

Think About Your Feelings and Attitudes to the Poem

1)   Pick 2 words or phrases that <u>stand out to you</u>. If none stand out, just pick 2 <u>unusual words or phrases</u>.

2)   Write these 2 words or phrases down. Then write about how they <u>make you feel</u>. If they don't make you feel anything, don't worry — just <u>make something up</u>, as long as it's not too stupid.

> **EXAMPLE**   The line "a father figure waits there, wants to set things straight", makes me worry about the safety of the person in the poem. The way this person has to sneak around suggests he or she is afraid of someone, making the father figure's intentions sound menacing and dangerous.

Themes — memory, imagery and mood...

Compare 'Homecoming' with other poems about the same themes: <u>memory</u> ('Before You Were Mine' p.44-45 and 'We Remember Your Childhood Well' p.46-47), <u>imagery</u> ('Tichborne's Elegy' p.14-15 and 'Havisham' p.36-37) and <u>mood</u> ('Elvis's Twin Sister' p.38-39).

58

Key Poem

November

The year moves to its end, like the old people's lives.

November

We walk to the ward from the badly parked car
with your grandma taking four short steps to our two.
We have brought her here to die and we know it.

Blunt statement that they can't ignore the sad truth of what's happening.

Uneven rhythm echoes her tiny steps.

Double meaning — "it's the right time", and also "time has done this to these people".

5   You check her towel, soap and family trinkets,
pare her nails, parcel her in the rough blankets
and she sinks down into her incontinence.

Strong image of how helpless she is.

Their whole bodies have stopped working properly.

It is time John. In their pasty bloodless smiles,
in their slack breasts, their stunned brains and their baldness,
and in us John: we are almost these monsters.

They will end up like this too. The matter-of-fact tone contrasts with the shocking word "monsters".

John's physically and emotionally broken by the experience.

10   You're shattered. You give me the keys and I drive
through the twilight zone, past the famous station
to your house, to numb ourselves with alcohol.

The darkness and run-down buildings surround them.

Inside, we feel the terror of the dusk begin.
Outside we watch the evening, failing again,
15   and we let it happen. We can say nothing.

The fading light represents the knowledge that they too are getting older.

They can't stop themselves from getting older.

There's only a small flicker of light.

Sometimes the sun spangles and we feel alive.
One thing we have to get, John, out of this life.

Tries to take something positive out of the day's events.

POEM DICTIONARY
pare — trim
incontinence — not being able to control bodily functions, like going to the toilet
twilight — fading light after sunset
twilight zone — a run-down industrial area

November Key Poem

The poet writes about taking the grandmother of a person called John to live in a <u>nursing home</u> or <u>hospital</u>. The poet and John both know she won't be coming out again. The poet writes as if he's talking to John, and describes their sad thoughts on the journey back.

You've Got to Know *What Happens in the Poem*

<u>Lines 1-6</u>	The poet and John help John's grandma settle in. She seems <u>weak</u> and <u>helpless</u>.
<u>Lines 7-9</u>	Other <u>old people</u> are described. They are pale and seemingly <u>lifeless</u>.
<u>Lines 10-15</u>	The poet and John go home. They feel really <u>depressed</u>, watching the night draw in.
<u>Lines 16-17</u>	The poet says that we should <u>make the most</u> of the chances we get to <u>live</u>.

Learn About the *Three Types of Language*

1) <u>DECAY</u> — There are lots of images of things <u>breaking down</u>, e.g. the <u>health</u> of the old people. The title of the poem suggests the cold weather is approaching, and strengthens the idea that the old people are in the <u>autumn years</u> of their lives.

2) <u>INEVITABILITY</u> — The poem is written in the <u>present tense</u>, as if it's happening now. This emphasises that you can't <u>avoid</u> growing old and dying — it's bound to happen eventually.

3) <u>DARKNESS</u> — The daylight fades away during the poem, suggesting the gradual approach of <u>death</u>. The gloomy setting also represents the poet's and John's <u>depressed thoughts</u>.

Remember the *Feelings and Attitudes in the Poem*

1) <u>HORROR</u> — The poet is <u>horrified</u> by the state of the old people.

2) <u>FEAR</u> — He's <u>depressed</u> and <u>frightened</u> by the thought of the same thing happening to him and everyone else (line 13).

3) <u>HELPLESSNESS</u> — He feels <u>helpless</u> to prevent an equally horrible end to his own life (line 15).

Think About *Your Feelings and Attitudes to the Poem*

1) Pick 2 words or phrases that <u>stand out to you</u>. If none stand out, just pick 2 <u>unusual words or phrases</u>.

2) Write these 2 words or phrases down. Then write about how they <u>make you feel</u>. If they don't make you feel anything, don't worry — just <u>make something up</u>, as long as it's not too stupid.

> **EXAMPLE** I find the poet's comment, "we are almost these monsters", very shocking. Describing old people as "monsters" makes them sound totally inhuman and disgusting. Also the fact that he is "almost" like them suggests the poet will inevitably end up the same way.

Themes — *death, attitudes to others, strong emotions...*

Compare 'November' to other poems on the same themes: <u>death</u> ('Tichborne's Elegy' p.14-15 and 'Ulysses' p.26-27), <u>attitudes towards other people</u> ('The Man He Killed' p.16-17 and 'Salome' p.42-43) and <u>strong emotions</u> ('Havisham' p.36-37 and 'On my first Sonne' p.6-7).

Kid

Kid

Batman, big shot, when you gave the order
to grow up, then let me loose to wander
leeward, freely through the wild blue yonder
as you liked to say, or ditched me, rather,
5   in the gutter ... well, I turned the corner.
Now I've scotched that 'he was like a father
to me' rumour, sacked it, blown the cover
on that 'he was like an elder brother'
story, let the cat out on that caper
10   with the married woman, how you took her
downtown on expenses in the motor.
Holy robin-redbreast-nest-egg-shocker!
Holy roll-me-over-in-the-clover,
I'm not playing ball boy any longer
15   Batman, now I've doffed that off-the-shoulder
Sherwood-Forest-green and scarlet number
for a pair of jeans and crew-neck jumper;
now I'm taller, harder, stronger, older.
Batman, it makes a marvellous picture:
20   you without a shadow, stewing over
chicken giblets in the pressure cooker,
next to nothing in the walk-in larder,
punching the palm of your hand all winter,
you baby, now I'm the real boy wonder.

Alliteration emphasises sarcasm and contempt.

His tone is bitter when he describes how he was deserted.

Combines the phrases "playing ball" and "ball boy" to stress how he used to do whatever Batman wanted.

Rhyme and rhythm make these words reflect his new strength and energy.

Imagines Batman eating basic, disgusting food on his own.

Batman claimed he was giving Robin his freedom.

Robin felt scared and alone.

Batman was supposed to catch criminals, but these phrases make it sound like he's the criminal.

These lines combine Robin's "holy" catchphrase with tabloid-headline style scandals.

Normal clothes show he's grown up and he's living in the real world now.

Without Robin, Batman's alone.

Gloats about Batman's loneliness and frustration.

Robin was always called the "boy wonder", but now it has new meaning — Robin's in charge now.

POEM DICTIONARY
leeward — towards the wind
scotched — put an end to
caper — a crime in a comic or film
on expenses — paid for by your employer
doffed — got rid of
giblets — the guts and insides of a chicken

Kid

This poem uses the superhero <u>Batman</u> and his sidekick <u>Robin</u> to stand for a young person who's been deserted by the person who was supposed to look after him. Now Robin is taking revenge, by showing that "Batman" wasn't such a hero after all. Holy poetry anthology!

You've Got to Know *What Happens in the Poem*

<u>Lines 1-5</u>	Robin (the narrator) is angry that Batman left him to <u>fend for himself</u> when he wasn't ready. But now Robin's <u>taking control</u> of his life.
<u>Lines 6-13</u>	Robin takes pleasure in revealing what Batman was <u>really like</u>. He <u>wasn't</u> a father figure to Robin as people had thought — he was taking out a <u>married woman</u> and claiming the money back from work.
<u>Lines 14-18</u>	Robin says he's not going to be Batman's <u>sidekick</u> any more. He's <u>grown up</u>, got rid of his silly costume and got some proper clothes.
<u>Lines 19-24</u>	Robin imagines Batman falling on hard times, and <u>gloats</u> when he pictures him <u>struggling</u>.

Learn About the *Three Types of Language*

1) <u>LANGUAGE ABOUT LONELINESS</u> — At first Robin describes <u>his own loneliness</u>, but by the end of the poem it's <u>Batman</u> who's <u>on his own</u>, in Robin's imagination at least.

2) <u>CLICHÉS</u> — There are a lot of commonly-used phrases and <u>clichés</u>, but they often <u>merge</u> together or end in an <u>unexpected</u> way. A lot of these phrases come from the <u>Batman</u> comics.

3) <u>BITTERNESS</u> and <u>SARCASM</u> — Robin's <u>bitter</u> and <u>annoyed</u> that everyone thinks Batman was so <u>great</u>. This is what makes him determined to get <u>revenge</u> by revealing the truth about him.

Remember the *Feelings and Attitudes in the Poem*

"I'm a bat, man."

1) <u>ANGER</u> — Robin is <u>angry</u> and <u>bitter</u> that Batman deserted him.

2) <u>DEFIANCE</u> — But he feels more <u>confident</u> now — he's <u>defiant</u> when he says he's "turned the corner".

3) <u>PRIDE</u> — Robin's <u>proud</u> of his new-found <u>independence</u>.

4) <u>PLEASURE</u> — He <u>enjoys</u> dishing the dirt on Batman, and <u>takes pleasure</u> from the idea of Batman being sad and alone.

Think About *Your Feelings and Attitudes to the Poem*

1) Pick 2 words or phrases that <u>stand out to you</u>. If none stand out, just pick 2 <u>unusual words or phrases</u>.

2) Write these 2 words or phrases down. Then write about how they <u>make you feel</u>. If they don't make you feel anything, don't worry — just <u>make something up</u>, as long as it's not too stupid.

> **EXAMPLE** When the Robin character says "I'm not playing ball boy any longer", I admire his determination. He feels very badly treated by "Batman", but instead of wallowing in self-pity, he has done something about it. I think that shows a lot of courage and self-belief.

Themes — *getting older, memory and characters...*

Compare 'Kid' with other poems about the same themes: <u>getting older</u> ('Mother, any distance...' p.52-53 and 'My father thought it...' p.54-55), <u>memory</u> ('My Last Duchess' p.22-23 and 'Before You Were Mine' p.44-45) and <u>characters</u> ('The Village Schoolmaster' p.28-29).

Those bastards in their mansions

from **Book of Matches**

Those bastards in their mansions:
to hear them shriek, you'd think
I'd poisoned the dogs and vaulted the ditches,
crossed the lawns in stocking feet and threadbare britches,
5 forced the door of one of the porches, and lifted
the gift of fire from the burning torches,

then given heat and light to streets and houses,
told the people how to ditch their cuffs and shackles,
armed them with the iron from their wrists and ankles.

10 Those lords and ladies in their palaces and castles,
they'd have me sniffed out by their beagles,
picked at by their eagles, pinned down, grilled
beneath the sun.

Me, I stick to the shadows, carry a gun.

Annotations:

- He's totally open about his hatred for rich people.
- Makes them sound whingeing and pathetic.
- They think he's sneaky.
- He imagines breaking into their homes.
- He seems to think revolution is a pretty good idea.
- The upper class seem very distant and different to him.
- This sounds scary, like he's waiting for his opportunity.
- Suggests wealth and privilege, and this is what he really seems to hate.
- Double meaning — "vault" means jump over, but a vault is also a place where rich people keep money.
- Another stereotype of rich houses. He suggests the ditches are there to keep him out.
- Stereotype of poverty.
- Suggests ordinary people are imprisoned by the rich.
- Stereotype that the upper class all hunt animals. He says they want to hunt him down in the same way.
- His intentions are far more violent than they imagined.

This poem has references to the story of Prometheus. In Greek mythology, Prometheus stole fire from the gods to give to mankind. As a punishment, he was chained to a rock where an eagle tore at his liver.

POEM DICTIONARY
britches — trousers worn to the knee or just below
beagles — a breed of dog used for hunting

Those bastards in their mansions

The person in this poem has really got it in for <u>rich people</u>. He says they treat him like he's trying to start a <u>revolution</u>. Turns out he's just lurking in the shadows. With a gun. So that's all right then.

You've Got to Know What Happens in the Poem

<u>Lines 1-6</u>   The person in the poem has a go at <u>rich people</u>. He says they treat him like he's a <u>criminal</u>.

<u>Lines 7-9</u>   He <u>denies</u> causing poor people to <u>revolt</u> — though it sounds like he'd like to.

<u>Lines 10-13</u>   He says that the rich want to <u>hunt him down</u> and imprison him.

<u>Line 14</u>   Rather than doing any of the things he's suspected of, he's <u>waiting for his chance</u> to strike.

Learn About the Three Types of Language

1) <u>STEREOTYPES</u> — His descriptions of rich and poor people are <u>simplified</u> and <u>exaggerated</u> — he sees the rich as living in big mansions, and imagines that they have a stereotyped image of the poor. He uses these <u>stereotypes</u> to emphasise how <u>different</u> rich people are from ordinary, working class people.

2) <u>REVOLUTIONARY LANGUAGE</u> — He sees ordinary, poor people as being <u>oppressed by the rich</u>. He says he <u>hasn't</u> been trying to start a <u>revolution</u>, i.e. getting the poor to take <u>power</u> from the rich. But the way he describes revolution suggests he thinks it would be a <u>good thing</u>.

3) <u>AGGRESSIVE LANGUAGE</u> — He has a lot of <u>violent</u>, <u>aggressive feelings</u> towards rich people. He describes the violent things he's been accused of, but <u>denies</u> they're true — until the last line.

Remember the Feelings and Attitudes in the Poem

"Go stop revolution, Rover."

1) <u>RESENTMENT</u> — The person in the poem <u>hates rich people</u>.

2) <u>OPPRESSION</u> — He says the rich <u>oppress ordinary people</u> — they control them with force.

3) <u>ANGER</u> — He's <u>angry</u> about the things he's been <u>wrongly accused</u> of.

4) <u>REVENGE</u> — He wants to have his <u>revenge</u> on rich people.

Think About Your Feelings and Attitudes to the Poem

1) Pick 2 words or phrases that <u>stand out to you</u>. If none stand out, just pick 2 <u>unusual words or phrases</u>.

2) Write these 2 words or phrases down. Then write about how they <u>make you feel</u>. If they don't make you feel anything, don't worry — just <u>make something up</u>, as long as it's not too stupid.

> EXAMPLE   When the person in the poem says "I stick to the shadows, carry a gun", it makes me feel both worried and excited. Having a gun shows he's plotting something very violent, which I find disturbing. But the way he waits in the shadows means we don't know when or how he will do it.

Themes — danger, attitudes to others and strong emotions

Compare 'Those bastards in their mansions' with other poems on the same themes: <u>danger</u> ('Education for Leisure' p.48-49 and 'Stealing' p.50-51), <u>attitudes towards other people</u> ('Hitcher' p.66-67) and <u>strong emotions</u> ('The Song of the Old Mother' p.8-9).

I've made out a will

from **Book of Matches**

I've made out a will; I'm leaving myself
to the National Health. I'm sure they can use
the jellies and tubes and syrups and glues,
the web of nerves and veins, the loaf of brains,
5 and assortment of fillings and stitches and wounds,
blood – a gallon exactly of bilberry soup –
the chassis or cage or cathedral of bone;
but not the heart, they can leave that alone.

They can have the lot, the whole stock:
10 the loops and coils and sprockets and springs and rods,
the twines and cords and strands,
the face, the case, the cogs and the hands,

but not the pendulum, the ticker;
leave that where it stops or hangs.

Annotations:

- Says his insides must be useful.
- Rhyming adds to the light-hearted tone.
- The exact amount reminds us of the will theme.
- Sounds like his body's a shop, and the parts are goods.
- Here, the body is like a car engine, with lots of complicated parts.
- We expect him to say he's leaving valuable items, but instead he leaves his body.
- His body is far from perfect.
- Funny way to describe the deep colour of blood.
- Reminds us of the saying "Your body is a temple" — you should look after it.
- Blunt tone makes his feelings clear.
- The body is just clothing — it's not important.
- The body is described like a clock.
- The poem ends on the serious subject of death.

POEM DICTIONARY
fillings — teeth fillings
bilberry — a type of fruit
chassis — the frame of a car
sprockets — wheels on a chain
pendulum — part of a clock which swings back and forth

I've made out a will

The poet has written a __will__ — but instead of saying who he's leaving his possessions to, he says he's leaving his __body__ to the NHS. It's quite funny, but has a serious point — he says the NHS can have everything but his heart, which is the only part of his body that's important to him.

You've Got to Know What Happens in the Poem

Lines 1-8   The poet describes all the different things in his __body__, in a disgusting but comical way. He says the National Health Service can have __everything__ apart from his __heart__.

Lines 9-12   He compares his body to an __engine__ (line 10), __clothes__ (line 11) and a __clock__ (line 12).

Lines 13-14   The poem ends on a more __serious__ note, by reminding us of the suddenness of __death__.

Learn About the Three Types of Language

1) __LANGUAGE RELATED TO WILLS__ — There are a few little __phrases__ thrown in which give the poem the feel of a __will__. This reinforces the theme of the poem.

2) __HUMOROUS LANGUAGE__ — There are quite a lot of __funny descriptions__, even though they're often about pretty __disgusting__ things like blood and guts. This allows the poet to talk about death, which could be a pretty depressing subject, in a __light-hearted__ way.

3) __METAPHORICAL LANGUAGE__ — The body is described as if it's various different things, such as an __engine__, a __clock__ and a __cathedral__. This helps the poet give a certain __impression__ of the body and its different parts.

Remember the Feelings and Attitudes in the Poem

Anyone for jelly?

1) __HUMOUR__ — The poet has a __light-hearted__ attitude towards his body.

2) __FEARLESSNESS__ — He's __not bothered__ about the prospect of __death__.

3) __SENTIMENTALITY__ — He has an emotional __attachment__ to his __heart__.

> The poet's feelings about his heart could refer to its connection to love — although he doesn't say this outright.

Think About Your Feelings and Attitudes to the Poem

1) Pick 2 words or phrases that __stand out to you__. If none stand out, just pick 2 __unusual words or phrases__.

2) Write these 2 words or phrases down. Then write about how they __make you feel__. If they don't make you feel anything, don't worry — just __make something up__, as long as it's not too stupid.

> __EXAMPLE__   I find the poet's description of "the jellies and tubes and syrups and glues" in his body sickening. It's a very unpleasant way of describing what people's bodies are made of.

Themes — death, imagery and the first person...

Compare 'I've made out a will' with other poems about the same themes: __death__ ('Tichborne's Elegy' p.14-15 and 'November' p.58-59), __imagery__ ('Sonnet 130' p.20-21 and 'Havisham' p.36-37) and use of the __first person__ ('Education for Leisure' p.48-49 and 'Homecoming' p.56-57).

Hitcher

Key Poem

Hitcher

The narrator is trying to get away from stress at work.

Before he kills the hitcher, the killer himself hitches a lift.

The hitcher is relaxed and dreamy, unlike the narrator.

The violence is shocking because it comes suddenly — there's no build-up to it.

Pretends he's being considerate.

Disturbing image, but his matter-of-fact tone suggests he's not bothered by it.

Makes fun of the hitcher's dreamy attitude.

The narrator's problems come to him via modern technology — the hitcher lives a simpler life.

Rhyming words emphasise pressure from work.

Romantic image of travelling.

He hits the hitcher several times — it's a savage attack.

Sounds like he's boasting.

Another connection between him and the hitcher, but it doesn't matter to him.

The rhyming here shows the narrator is more relaxed than at the start of the poem.

I'd been tired, under
the weather, but the ansaphone kept screaming:
One more sick-note, mister, and you're finished. Fired.
I thumbed a lift to where the car was parked.
5   A Vauxhall Astra. It was hired.

I picked him up in Leeds.
He was following the sun to west from east
with just a toothbrush and the good earth for a bed. The truth,
he said, was blowin' in the wind,
10   or round the next bend.

I let him have it
on the top road out of Harrogate – once
with the head, then six times with the krooklok
in the face – and didn't even swerve.
15   I dropped it into third

and leant across
to let him out, and saw him in the mirror
bouncing off the kerb, then disappearing down the verge.
We were the same age, give or take a week.
20   He'd said he liked the breeze

to run its fingers
through his hair. It was twelve noon.
The outlook for the day was moderate to fair.
Stitch that, I remember thinking,
25   you can walk from there.

POEM DICTIONARY
thumbed — hitched
krooklok — device used to prevent car theft
verge — slope at the side of a road
moderate — mild

Section Three — Simon Armitage

Hitcher

Key Poem

The chap in this poem isn't an awfully nice fella. He picks up a <u>hitch-hiker</u> — ok so far — then duffs him up, chucks him out of his car while it's still going and <u>leaves him for dead</u>. And the moral of the story is: if you're in Leeds, get the bus.

You've Got to Know What Happens in the Poem

<u>Lines 1-5</u>   The narrator was feeling <u>under pressure</u> as he hitched a lift to the car he'd hired.

<u>Lines 6-10</u>   He describes picking a <u>hitch-hiker</u> up, and the <u>easy-going</u> lifestyle the hitcher was leading.

<u>Lines 11-18</u>   He tells us he <u>beat up</u> the hitcher while he was still driving, then <u>pushed him out</u> of the car.

<u>Lines 19-25</u>   He jokes that the <u>weather's nice</u> so the hitcher can <u>walk</u> the rest of the way.

Learn About the Four Types of Language

1) <u>CONTRASTS</u> — The simple, <u>relaxed</u> life of the hitcher contrasts with the <u>stress</u> the narrator feels.

2) <u>VIOLENT LANGUAGE</u> — The narrator describes quite <u>graphically</u> how he <u>attacked</u> the hitcher. His descriptions are particularly shocking because of the <u>casual tone</u> of voice he uses.

3) <u>INAPPROPRIATE REMARKS</u> — He makes some pretty <u>nasty comments</u> and <u>sick jokes</u> about the assault. He <u>makes fun</u> of the hitcher for his easy-going <u>lifestyle</u>.

4) <u>LINKS</u> — There are some <u>similarities</u> between the narrator and the hitcher.

Remember the Feelings and Attitudes in the Poem

One more sick note Mr...

1) <u>STRESS</u> — At the start of the poem, the narrator feels irritable, ill and <u>under pressure</u>.

2) <u>DETACHMENT</u> — His matter-of-fact tone shows he <u>doesn't feel bad</u> about what he does.

3) <u>JEALOUSY</u> — He <u>envies</u> the hitch-hiker's relaxed lifestyle and hates him for it.

4) <u>SPITE</u> — His nasty joke at the end suggests he takes a <u>sick pleasure</u> from killing the hitch-hiker.

Think About Your Feelings and Attitudes to the Poem

1) Pick 2 words or phrases that <u>stand out to you</u>. If none stand out, just pick 2 <u>unusual words or phrases</u>.

2) Write these 2 words or phrases down. Then write about how they <u>make you feel</u>. If they don't make you feel anything, don't worry — just <u>make something up</u>, as long as it's not too stupid.

> **EXAMPLE** When the narrator describes the hitcher "bouncing off the kerb, then disappearing down the verge", I feel shocked. This is a horrible image. Even though he knows he has probably killed the hitcher, the narrator describes it as if it is a perfectly normal sight.

Themes — mood, evil and attitudes towards other people...

Compare 'Hitcher' with other poems about the same themes: <u>mood</u> ('Havisham' p.36-37 and 'Education for Leisure' p.48-49), <u>evil</u> ('My Last Duchess' p.22-23 and 'The Laboratory' p.30-31) and <u>attitudes towards other people</u> ('The Song of the Old Mother' p.8-9 and 'Stealing' p.50-51).

Section Three — Simon Armitage

Death

Death is something people feel _emotional_ about — so it's a good theme for poetry.

1) The death of a loved one causes _grief_ and a sense of _loss_.
2) Everyone dies — it's something we need to _prepare_ for.
3) Deaths caused by _war, crime or execution_ can seem like a pointless waste of life.

Some Poets write about Killing and Murder

Education for Leisure (Pages 48-49)

1) The poet writes from the point of view of a _psychopath_ who's planning to "kill something".
2) The character usually has a _dull life_ — feeling "ignored" and suffering from "boredom".
3) The character gets _obsessed_ with the _power of killing_. It makes their life feel more _exciting_. They imagine themselves as a "genius" and a "superstar".
4) At the end of the poem, the character seems to _threaten the reader_: "I touch your arm."

The Man He Killed (Pages 16-17)

1) In this poem, a soldier talks about a man he _killed during a battle_. He points out the _irony_ that if he had met the man in other circumstances, they might have been friends.
2) He imagines that the man he killed was rather _like himself_. Even though officially the man was his enemy, there might not have been anything bad about him.
3) The poem points out how _foolish and wasteful_ the _killing in war_ is: "You shoot a fellow down / You'd treat if met where any bar is".

Maybe we should just go for a pint.

Death can be Depressing

On my first Sonne (Pages 6-7)

1) The poet expresses the _grief_ he feels over the _loss of a child_: "Farewell, thou child of my right hand, and joy".
2) The poet tries to find something _positive_ in his son's death — that at least the boy has escaped many of life's troubles and old age.
3) He pays _tribute_ to his son by saying he was "his best piece of poetrie" — his best work. He vows never to love anything so much again, in case he loses it.

November (Pages 58-59)

1) Seeing the _old people_ makes the poet think about his _own death_.
2) The old people appear to be very _close to death_ — their "pasty bloodless smiles" and "stunned brains" suggest that some parts of their bodies are _already_ dead.
3) The thought of death _depresses_ the poet — "we feel the terror of the dusk begin."
4) But at the end he says, "sometimes the sun spangles", and this makes him _determined_ to get as much out of life as possible _before he dies_.

This topic's a bit bleak...

Other poems which talk about death are: 'Tichborne's Elegy' (p.14-15), 'The Laboratory' (p.30-31), 'Salome' (p.42-43) and 'Hitcher' (p.66-67). They fall into two camps — 1) poets feeling awful about people dying in real life, and 2) poets writing from the point of view of a crazed killer.

Parent/Child Relationships

Family arguments — a great source of poetic inspiration.

> 1) The parent/child relationship is <u>central</u> to most people's lives.
> 2) Parent/child relationships often <u>change</u> as people grow older.
> 3) Some children struggle to be <u>free</u> from their parents.

Parents Find it Hard to Let Go

Mother, any distance (Pages 52-53)

1) The person in this poem is moving into his <u>own house</u>. He's becoming <u>independent</u> from his mum.
2) His mum helps him <u>measure</u> things. The tape measure, "unreeling / years between us", becomes a metaphor for all their <u>shared memories</u> and history.
3) His mother finds it <u>difficult to let go</u> of him completely: "your fingertips still pinch / the last one-hundredth of an inch".
4) At the end, he faces up to <u>life without his mum</u>. He's ready "to fall or fly".

The Affliction of Margaret (Pages 10-11)

1) The woman in the poem hasn't heard from her son for <u>7 years</u>.
2) We see how <u>upset</u> the mother is at not knowing whether her son is <u>dead or alive</u>.
3) She's <u>desperate</u> to hear from him, whatever has happened to him: "Oh find me, prosperous or undone!"
4) She describes her son as if he's almost <u>perfect</u>: "He was among the prime in worth".

Children's Views of their Parents Change Over Time

My father thought it bloody queer (Pages 54-55)

1) The poet remembers his <u>father's anger</u> and <u>sarcasm</u> when he "rolled home with a ring of silver" in his ear. He was hurt and upset by his father's reaction.
2) When the earring became <u>sore and painful</u>, he started to realise his father might have been right.
3) Now the poet's older, he finds himself <u>giving the same advice</u> as his father did: "*If I were you, / I'd take it out and leave it out next year.*"

Parents Give Things Up for their Children

Tidy your room, luv.

Before You Were Mine (Pages 44-45)

1) The poet imagines her <u>mother</u> as a <u>glamorous young woman</u> in the 1950s, looking and behaving like "Marilyn".
2) She likes to think of her mother as a bit of a <u>rebel</u> who <u>put pleasure first</u>. She imagines her staying out late, not caring that she would get "a hiding" when she came home.
3) She remembers as a child, playing with her mum's high-heeled shoes, "<u>relics</u>" of her fun-loving past, and her mum teaching her to "*Cha cha cha*" on the way back from Church.
4) She realises what her mother has <u>given up</u> since her <u>birth</u>. With the "loud, possessive yell" of a <u>young baby</u>, she took over her mum's life.

Everyone starts off as a squalling baby...

Other poems which describe parent/child relationships are 'On my first Sonne' (p.6-7), 'We Remember Your Childhood Well' (p.46-47) and 'Kid' (p.60-61).

Danger

Some people are <u>scared</u> by danger — others get a <u>kick out of it</u>.

> 1) Danger can come from <u>nature</u>, e.g. storms, earthquakes and floods.
>
> 2) Danger can also be <u>caused by people</u> — through aggression and violence.
>
> 3) Some people find danger and risk-taking <u>exciting</u> (we don't endorse this attitude...).

People can Find Themselves in <u>Dangerous Situations</u>

The Little Boy Lost and The Little Boy Found (Pages 12-13)

1) The little boy is <u>helpless</u> on his own — "the mire was deep".
2) The danger is <u>avoided</u> when <u>God</u> appears, "like his father in white".
3) Blake uses the story to make his <u>religious message</u> clear — he says we're <u>lost without God</u>.

Patrolling Barnegat (Pages 18-19)

1) The poem describes a small band of watchmen patrolling the beach during a <u>fierce storm</u>.
2) The storm is described as very <u>powerful</u>: "Waves, air, midnight, their savagest trinity lashing". It is an <u>uncontrollable</u> part of nature: "Wild, wild the storm".
3) The storm is <u>dangerous</u> — out to sea the watchmen wonder if they can see a <u>wrecked ship</u>: "is that a wreck? is the red signal flaring?".

Some Poets write about <u>Dangerous People</u>

Hitcher (Pages 66-67)

1) The poem is written from the point of view of a man who attacks a hitch-hiker.
2) As the story unfolds, it becomes clear that the narrator is a <u>dangerous criminal</u>.
3) The hitch-hiker is <u>unaware of the danger</u> he's in. He talks happily to the narrator about his life and his hopes: "The truth, / he said, was blowin' in the wind".
4) The attack is <u>brutal and shocking</u>, especially because the narrator doesn't seem shocked by it: "I let him have it / on the top road out of Harrogate".

Danger and Risk-Taking can be <u>Exciting</u>

This page is just so darn depressing...

Stealing (Pages 50-51)

1) The poem is written from the point of view of a <u>young thief</u>.
2) There <u>isn't any point</u> to the thief's law-breaking: "I steal things I don't need. I joy-ride cars / to nowhere".
3) The only reason the thief does it is for the "<u>thrill</u>" — the thief describes the <u>excitement</u> he/she feels from standing in "A stranger's bedroom. Mirrors. I sigh like this — *Aah.*"
4) When he/she isn't stealing, the thief feels <u>bored</u>: "Mostly I'm so bored I could eat myself."

People do strange things for kicks...

This is a bit of a grim topic: people being frightened and getting hurt. If you want more of this doleful stuff, then have a look at these poems: 'The Laboratory' (p.30-31), 'Education for Leisure' (p.48-49) and 'Those bastards in their mansions' (p.62-63).

Attitudes Towards Other People

Poems are often about the poets' attitudes and feelings towards other people.

> 1) Some poets write about <u>positive</u> attitudes and feelings towards other people.
> 2) Some poets write about <u>negative</u> or <u>violent</u> attitudes towards other people.
> 3) Sometimes poets write about how their attitudes towards other people <u>change</u>.

Poems can be about Positive Attitudes towards Others

Anne Hathaway (Pages 40-41)

1) The poem is written from the <u>point of view of Shakespeare's wife</u>, remembering her <u>dead husband</u>.
2) Her <u>attitude</u> towards him is very <u>loving</u> and <u>affectionate</u>. She describes him as "My living laughing love", as if he is still alive. The word "laughing" shows how much she enjoyed his company.
3) She has <u>fond memories</u> of how he made her feel. She describes how spending time with him was like going to a magical land: "a spinning world / of forests, castles, torchlight".
4) Even now he's dead, she <u>won't forget him</u>: she carries the memories in "the casket of my widow's head".

Poems can show Negative Attitudes towards Others

Those bastards in their mansions (Pages 62-63)

1) The character in the poem <u>hates</u> rich, upper class "bastards".
2) He has a <u>stereotyped</u> view of them — "Those lords and ladies in their palaces and castles".
3) He sees rich people as <u>bullies</u> who would "have me sniffed out by their beagles".
4) He also suggests that they're a bit <u>pathetic</u>, as they "shriek" about him breaking into their houses.

Kid (Pages 60-61)

1) The narrator <u>hates Batman</u> because he "ditched" him when he was young.
2) The narrator thinks other people had a <u>false impression</u> of Batman. He says he's "scotched that 'he was like a father / to me' rumour" and shown everyone what Batman's <u>really like</u>.
3) The narrator sees Batman as <u>selfish</u> for abandoning him. He also sees him as <u>immoral</u> — he was taking a married woman "downtown on expenses in the motor".
4) At the end of the poem, the narrator portrays Batman as a <u>loser</u>, living on his own <u>eating rubbish</u>: "you without a shadow, stewing over / chicken giblets in the pressure cooker".

"Mad, moi?"

The Laboratory (Pages 30-31)

1) The woman in the poem feels <u>really angry</u> towards her <u>lover/husband</u> and his <u>new mistress</u>. She thinks they've made a <u>fool</u> of her: "they laugh, laugh at me".
2) She's determined to get <u>revenge</u> and wants to use poison to <u>kill</u> the mistress in a <u>painful way</u>: "Let death be felt and the proof remain".
3) Through killing his mistress, she hopes to <u>hurt</u> her lover/husband as well: "He is sure to remember her dying face!"

Anger, resentment, love, lust, hate, jealousy, contempt...

Poems which show characters' attitudes towards other people include: 'Stealing' (p.50-51), 'Hitcher' (p.66-67) and 'The Song of the Old Mother' (p.8-9).

Love

There are a few poems on the good old-fashioned theme of love in this anthology, but <u>not</u> <u>many</u> of them are <u>romantic</u>. Some of them are about love between people in families, some of them describe love of nature, or even love of crime...

> 1) Some poets write about <u>romantic love</u>.
> 2) Poets also write about loving their <u>friends</u> and <u>family</u>.
> 3) Some poets write about their love of <u>nature</u>, or a particular <u>place</u> or <u>hobby</u>.

Some Poems are about *Romantic Love*

Sonnet 130 (Pages 20-21)

1) This poem is a <u>sonnet</u> (it's 14 lines long). Sonnet form is often used for <u>love poetry</u>.
2) In the first part of the poem, Shakespeare <u>goes against the reader's expectations</u> of a love sonnet. He's <u>pretty rude</u> about his mistress, e.g. he says her "eyes are nothing like the sun", her hair is like "black wires" and her breath "reeks".
3) On line 9, he says "I love to hear her speak". This is the <u>first hint</u> that he <u>does love his mistress</u>.
4) In the last two lines, the tone changes. Shakespeare declares that his mistress is <u>just as wonderful</u> as <u>any woman</u> who's <u>praised</u> with <u>silly compliments</u>: "I think my love as rare / As any she belied with false compare."

Anne Hathaway (Pages 40-41)

1) This poem is a <u>sonnet</u>, an old-fashioned form of love poem.
2) The poem is written from the point of view of Anne Hathaway, describing the love between her and her <u>husband</u> Shakespeare, before he died.
3) The love between them was almost <u>too good to be true</u>. Anne uses <u>romantic</u>, <u>magical words</u> to describe it: "My lover's words / were shooting stars".
4) She says their love was "Romance / and drama played by touch, by scent, by taste" — their love was so <u>passionate</u> she felt as if they were characters in one of her husband's <u>plays</u>.

Some Poems are about Love of *Places* or *Nature*

Sonnet (Pages 34-35)

1) The poet describes how much he <u>loves the countryside</u> in <u>summer</u>.
2) He starts three lines with the phrase "<u>I love</u>" which emphasises his feelings.
3) He describes the countryside in a very <u>positive way</u>, using words like "beaming", "happy" and "bright" to show how much he likes it.

Inversnaid (Pages 32-33)

1) The poet describes a place with <u>wild, natural scenery</u>, with a "darksome burn" rolling through the hills.
2) In the final stanza, the poet makes an appeal for places like this to be left alone. He <u>loves</u> the "<u>wilderness</u>" and wants it to survive.

"Who cares about boys? I love shrubbery..."

Some poets love Wolverhampton Wanderers...

The poems in this anthology are pretty bleak — there aren't many about love. Other poems you could look at are: 'On my first Sonne' (p.6-7), 'The Affliction of Margaret' (p.10-11), 'Mother, any distance' (p.52-53), and... no, that's it.

Memory

Many poems are based around memories — of <u>people</u>, <u>events</u> and <u>feelings</u>.

> 1) Memories can be associated with many <u>different feelings</u>, e.g. pride, shame, joy or anger.
> 2) People sometimes <u>block out bad memories</u>.
> 3) Memories can be <u>unreliable</u> — you might remember things differently from how they actually happened.

Memories can be Unreliable and Confusing

Homecoming (Pages 56-57)

1) This poem is deliberately <u>ambiguous</u>. It encourages the reader to "Think" in the first line, and then presents a <u>series of images</u>, many of which seem to be from the <u>past</u>.
2) The clearest story is about a mother getting angry with her child — the child goes to bed angry and then sneaks off at night.
3) The poem <u>plays around with time</u>. The poet says he's there the night the person sneaks out, but there isn't any contact between them "because it's sixteen years or so before we'll meet."
4) The poet says the person should "<u>Retrace</u> that walk towards the garden gate". This suggests the <u>homecoming</u> of the poem's title. Maybe the child who sneaked away is returning home as an adult.

We Remember Your Childhood Well (Pages 46-47)

1) This poem is about someone telling someone else that his or her <u>memories</u> are <u>wrong</u>.
2) It seems likely that there is a <u>reason</u> why the memories are being denied — perhaps to cover up mistreatment or abuse that happened in the past.
3) The memories are only <u>hinted</u> at, which makes us think the <u>worst</u> about what happened, e.g. the phrase "Nobody forced you" sounds really sinister.

The Village Schoolmaster (Pages 28-29)

1) The poet points out the "<u>straggling fence</u>" next to where the school was. This makes him remember the <u>schoolmaster</u>.
2) The schoolmaster was "A man severe" — he <u>doesn't</u> sound particularly <u>friendly</u>. But he had bags of <u>knowledge</u> and a wide range of <u>skills</u>.
3) Memories of the schoolmaster are <u>unclear</u> in places, e.g. the poet says "the story ran that he could gauge", suggesting no-one was quite <u>sure</u> about him.

Some Memories inspire Pride and Affection

Ulysses (Pages 26-27)

1) Ulysses has returned to his home of Ithaca after years spent away. He finds normal life <u>boring</u> and wants to return to travelling and adventure.
2) Ulysses has <u>strong memories</u> of the <u>glory</u> of his former life. He remembers the "drunk delight of battle" and all that he has "seen and known".
3) In the past, he became <u>famous</u> and had an <u>impact on events</u>. He says, "I am a part of all that I have met".
4) He's <u>proud</u> of his achievements. Memories of his past glory inspire him to go travelling again: "I cannot rest from travel: I will drink / Life to the lees".

"Give me a sword and I'll show you a thing or two."

I remember it well...

"Memories, like the corners of my mind..." How does the rest of that song go? Ah well. Another poem which deals with memories is 'Before You Were Mine' (p.44-45). And don't forget it.

Evil

Evil is a good subject for poems because it's <u>dramatic</u> and <u>extreme</u>.

> 1) Some characters seem to kill just for <u>fun</u>.
>
> 2) Others become <u>obsessed</u> with <u>revenge</u>, and will do anything to get it.
>
> 3) Some characters appear quite <u>normal</u>, but give us little <u>glimpses</u> that they're not quite the ticket.

Some Characters are Openly Evil

The Laboratory (Pages 30-31)

1) The woman in this poem suspects her husband or lover has been <u>unfaithful</u> to her.
2) She's determined to get <u>revenge</u> by <u>poisoning</u> the other woman.
3) She's very <u>nasty</u> — she's prepared to <u>murder</u> the other woman just to <u>get her own back</u> on her husband. She sounds <u>pleased</u> when she says "He is sure to remember her dying face!"

Hitcher (Pages 66-67)

1) The narrator's <u>attitude</u> to the crime is <u>shocking</u> — he sounds calm when he describes it, rather than angry or worked up.
2) The nature of the violence is <u>horrifying</u> — he headbutts him, then hits him "six times with the krooklok / in the face".
3) He <u>makes fun</u> of the hitcher's attitude after attacking him: "He'd said he liked the breeze / to run its fingers / through his hair."

Some Characters Gradually Reveal their Evil Side

My Last Duchess (Pages 22-23)

1) The Duke is showing a guest a <u>portrait</u> of his <u>dead wife</u>. He seems <u>pleasant</u> and <u>polite</u>.
2) But we gradually realise there's something <u>fishy</u> about him. He starts to <u>criticise</u> the Duchess for the way she acted: "her looks went everywhere".
3) The Duke says the Duchess treated him <u>no better</u> than anyone else — he seems really <u>jealous</u>.
4) It sounds <u>suspicious</u> when he tells his guest: "I gave commands; / Then all smiles stopped together." This makes it sound like he had his wife <u>murdered</u> just because he didn't like her <u>flirting</u> with other men.

Salome (Pages 42-43)

1) The woman in this poem has <u>cut off a man's head</u>.
2) She seems <u>mildly regretful</u> at first, but we think this is because she's <u>slept with a stranger</u>.
3) When it turns out she's actually <u>beheaded</u> the man, we read what she's said in a different way. She says she'd "done it before" and she'll "do it again" — she's a <u>serial murderer</u>.
4) She <u>can't remember</u> who the man is: "a head on the pillow beside me – whose? – / what did it matter?"

I call him "Mini-Simon-Armitage"...

Yep, this anthology's certainly got a dark side. Other poems about evil are: 'Havisham' (p.36-37) and 'Education for Leisure' (p.48-49). But remember — don't have nightmares.

Getting Older

This theme falls into two camps: poems about growing up, and poems about ageing.

> 1) <u>Growing up</u> and living separately from your parents can be a <u>difficult</u> time.
> 2) <u>Growing old</u> and realising you've not got much time left can be <u>depressing</u>.

Growing Up can be a Difficult Time

Mother, any distance (Pages 52-53)

1) The character in this poem is <u>moving into a new house</u> for the first time.
2) He asks his <u>mum</u> to help him <u>measure the new house</u>. His mum stands at the bottom of the stairs holding a tape measure as her son walks up the stairs, holding the other end.
3) This situation is used as a <u>metaphor</u> for the character <u>moving away</u> from his mum. For a long time, his mother keeps hanging onto the end of the tape measure ("your fingertips still pinch / the last one-hundredth of an inch") — this represents the way she is <u>clinging on to her son</u>.
4) There comes a point when the character needs to <u>let go</u> of the tape measure, because it won't stretch any further. He has to "fall or fly" <u>without his mum</u> there to help him.

Kid (Pages 60-61)

1) The character in this poem feels that he was <u>let down</u> by the person who was supposed to look after him when he was young.
2) He says he was given "<u>the order / to grow up</u>" — expected to be independent before he was ready.
3) The character says he's now grown up and <u>made a success of himself</u>: "now I'm taller, harder, stronger, older." But he's <u>still</u> <u>bitter</u> about what happened when he was growing up.

Growing Old Isn't Much Fun Either

Ulysses (Pages 26-27)

1) Ulysses has returned home as a <u>hero</u> after 10 years <u>travelling back from war</u>, to rule over his people.
2) He's <u>bored</u> of being "an idle king" though, and wants to <u>continue his adventures</u> until he dies.
3) He knows he's <u>not as strong and fit</u> as he used to be, and he's aware that <u>death</u> isn't far away. But this <u>doesn't put him off</u> — he tells his crew that he is still "strong in will".
4) Ulysses <u>isn't</u> prepared to just <u>fade away</u> as he gets older. He wants to "drink / Life to the lees".

November (Pages 58-59)

1) The narrator finds the <u>old people</u> depressing to look at — their "pasty bloodless smiles" make them seem <u>almost dead</u> already.
2) He realises that he and John will soon be <u>old</u> too — "we are almost these monsters".
3) The thought of growing old <u>scares</u> him witless — "we feel the terror of the dusk begin."
4) He knows there's <u>nothing</u> he can do to avoid getting old and dying, but says it's important to <u>make the most</u> out of the times when "we feel alive".

"Oh no! I'm going to die!"

This page is dedicated to Adrian Mole Aged 13 and ¾...

Other poems about getting older are: 'Before You Were Mine' (p.44-45) and 'My father thought it bloody queer' (p.54-55). That's it for poets' ideas, attitudes and feelings. Phew.

Strong Emotions

Poets often show strong emotions in their poems — either their own emotions, or those of the people they are writing about. Strong emotions are things like love, hate, anger, jealousy and joy.

1) Poems are often about <u>personal</u> subjects, which the poet has strong emotions about.

2) Poems about <u>difficult situations</u> often contain strong emotions, e.g. poems about death or danger.

3) Poets can show strong emotions through the <u>language they use</u>.

Poems about <u>Difficult Situations</u> show Strong Emotions

On my first Sonne (Pages 6-7)

1) The poet <u>loved</u> his son and was very <u>proud</u> of him — he calls him his "best piece of poetrie".

2) He's <u>devastated</u> by his son's death, but he's also <u>grateful</u> for the time he had with him — "Seven yeeres tho'wert lent to me, and I thee pay."

3) Jonson sees life as <u>painful</u>. He suggests people are <u>better off dead</u>, as they don't have to suffer the pain of getting old — he asks: "why / Will man lament the state he should envie?"

Tichborne's Elegy (Pages 14-15)

1) This poem was written as the poet was <u>waiting for his execution</u> in the Tower of London.

2) The poet feels huge <u>sadness</u> and <u>bitterness</u> about his coming execution.

3) Throughout the poem, he keeps pointing out the <u>bitter irony</u> of his situation: even though he is young and healthy, his life is coming to an end: "My fruit is fallen, and yet my leaves are green".

4) He feels <u>angry</u> about the way his life is going to be <u>wasted</u>. Instead of being able to enjoy his life, it's going to be cut short: "My prime of youth is but a frost of cares."

Poems can Include <u>Mixed Emotions</u>

Havisham (Pages 36-37)

1) Havisham has very strong <u>mixed emotions</u> about the man who rejected her on her wedding day. She calls him "Beloved sweetheart bastard".

2) She's extremely <u>angry</u> and <u>bitter</u>, and wants to "strangle" him.

3) It's years since he rejected her, but she <u>can't let go</u> — "I stink and remember." She's <u>obsessed</u>.

4) She also desperately wants him to be there, and has <u>sexual fantasies</u> about "the lost body".

November (Pages 58-59)

1) This poem describes an elderly woman being taken to a care home. The poet feels <u>guilty</u> about putting the woman into care: "We have brought her here to die and we know it."

2) The poet's <u>feelings</u> about the elderly people in the care home are <u>mixed</u>.

3) On the one hand, the poet seems <u>disgusted</u> by the elderly people, describing them as almost <u>inhuman</u>. For example, he describes their "pasty bloodless smiles" and their "stunned brains".

4) He sounds <u>frightened</u> and <u>depressed</u> by old age, and the fact that he can do nothing to stop it happening. Nightfall is used as a <u>metaphor</u> for old age, because they're both inevitable: "we let it happen. We can say nothing."

Strong emotions are dramatic and fascinating...

Poems are often about personal or dramatic events — no wonder they're emotional. 'The Affliction of Margaret' (p.10-11) and 'Kid' (p.60-61) are also good examples of this theme.

Use of the First Person

If the poet writes in the <u>first person</u>, they use words like "<u>I</u>" and "<u>me</u>", rather than "she" and "him."

1) Writing in the first person allows the poet to use their voice <u>directly</u>.
2) This allows them to talk about their personal <u>thoughts and feelings</u>.
3) The first person lets us see things from the poet or character's <u>point of view</u>.

Writing in the First Person can Express Personal Feelings

Anne Hathaway (Pages 40-41)

1) The poet imagines Anne Hathaway's <u>feelings</u> after her husband dies.
2) The use of the first person makes the poem sound <u>loving</u> and <u>tender</u> — for example when she says, "My lover's words / were shooting stars" and "My living laughing love".
3) Using the first person emphasises how <u>personal</u> the feelings described in the poem are. It's about memories of a relationship — the kind of stuff other people wouldn't know about.

My father thought it bloody queer (Pages 54-55)

1) The poet uses the first person to show the <u>pain</u> he felt from having his ear pierced, and how <u>upset</u> he felt by his father's reaction.
2) He says he <u>hadn't dared</u> to "drive a needle through the skin". This shows he wasn't very courageous about it, and makes his attempt to be rebellious look a bit <u>silly</u>.
3) He shows that his father's mocking reaction <u>still bothers him</u>, as he describes "my own voice breaking like a tear" when he finds himself saying the same things his dad said to him.

Sonnet (Pages 34-35)

1) This poem is about how much the poet loves the <u>countryside in summer</u>.
2) Three lines of the poem start with "<u>I love</u>", repeating his strong feelings.

Yup, it's lovely out here.

Writing in the First Person can be Persuasive

The Man He Killed (Pages 16-17)

1) This poem makes a point about the <u>violence and foolishness of war</u> — how people who could be friends kill each other because they are on different sides.
2) Hardy writes in the first person from the <u>point of view of a soldier</u> who has fought in a war. This <u>increases the strength</u> of the message because the character knows what he's talking about.
3) Using the first person makes it sound as if the character is <u>talking directly</u> to the reader: "I shot him dead because – / Because he was my foe". This makes the poem's message more <u>convincing</u>.

The Song of the Old Mother (Pages 8-9)

1) The message of the poem is about how <u>harsh</u> life is for many <u>old people</u>.
2) The poet writes in the first person, from the point of view of an old woman.
3) The character of the woman <u>talks directly to the reader</u> about her situation. She describes her <u>list of chores</u>, starting early "in the dawn" and not stopping till the stars are out. She contrasts this with the "idleness" of young people.

The first person lets the poet speak directly to the reader...

'Stealing' (p.50-51) and 'Mother, any distance' (p.52-53) also use the first person. It makes a big difference to the effect of a poem, as it lets the poet talk personally — poems like 'The Man He Killed' would lose a lot of impact if it was just "he" or "she" instead of "I".

Characters

Most poets write about people — apart from the nature-loving, obsessed-with-the-countryside brigade.

1) Many poems are about a particular character — his/her <u>personality</u>, <u>actions</u> and <u>emotions</u>.
2) The characters in a poem can be <u>real</u> or completely <u>made-up</u>.
3) Sometimes the main character is the <u>poet</u> him/herself.
4) Sometimes an important character isn't actually present in the poem — they're just <u>talked about</u> by the narrator.

Characters can be Portrayed Negatively

Kid (Pages 60-61)

1) The poem is addressed to a character who was a <u>father-figure</u> to the poet in his childhood.
2) The narrator says that he hero-worshipped this character but was <u>badly let down</u> by him — ditched "in the gutter".
3) Even now the narrator is older, he's <u>still bitter</u> about the way he was treated. He enjoys thinking about the character being unhappy and alone: "punching the palm of your hand all winter".
4) He refers to the character <u>sarcastically</u> as "<u>Batman, big shot</u>". He used to think the character was a big hero, but it turned out he was much more ordinary.

Havisham (Pages 36-37)

1) The character in this poem is based on a character called <u>Miss Havisham</u>, in Charles Dickens' novel "<u>Great Expectations</u>". She was stood up on her wedding day and went a bit <u>crazy</u>.
2) In the poem, she has extremely <u>violent</u> thoughts about the bloke who rejected her, but she's also <u>desperate</u> for him to come back. She's <u>obsessed</u> with the rejection she suffered.
3) We can see her <u>confusion</u> in the opening line, when she calls him "Beloved sweetheart bastard."
4) Overall, she's very <u>bitter</u> and <u>violent</u> — she wants "a male corpse for a long slow honeymoon", showing she's lost control.

Sometimes a Key Character is Absent

The Affliction of Margaret (Pages 10-11)

1) In this poem, a woman called Margaret worries about what has happened to her son who disappeared seven years ago. Even though we <u>never meet the son</u>, he is an <u>important character</u> in the poem.
2) Margaret's opinion of her son is very <u>loving and positive</u>. She says that he was "among the prime in worth, / An object beauteous to behold".

My Last Duchess (Pages 22-23)

1) In the poem, a rich man looks at a painting of his <u>dead wife</u> and describes what she was like.
2) The <u>character</u> of the dead wife is described in a lot of detail — but all through the <u>eyes of her husband</u>, who may have had her <u>killed</u>. We never hear her side of the story.
3) The Duke says his wife made him angry because she <u>smiled and blushed</u> at everyone, rather than just at him. There is a suggestion that she was <u>unfaithful</u> to him: "she liked whate'er / She looked on, and her looks went everywhere."

Characters are just the people in a poem...

Other poems with interesting characters include: 'Ulysses' (p.26-27), 'The Village Schoolmaster' (p.28-29), 'Salome' (p.42-43), 'Education for Leisure' (p.48-49) and 'Hitcher' (p.66-67).

Imagery

The way a poet writes can make you form a picture in your head of what's being described — this is called "imagery". Two common forms of imagery are <u>metaphors</u> and <u>similes</u> (see glossary).

> 1) Imagery helps the reader <u>imagine</u> the situations, characters and emotions described in a poem.
>
> 2) Imagery often uses <u>comparisons</u> to describe something, e.g. "She ran like the wind."

Imagery can be used to Describe People

I've made out a will (Pages 64-65)

1) The poet gives a lot of fairly <u>disgusting</u> but <u>funny</u> descriptions of the <u>insides</u> of his <u>body</u>.
2) The "jellies and tubes and syrups and glues" sound pretty <u>horrible</u>. They also make it sound like his body is made up of <u>food</u>, with "bilberry soup" in his veins instead of <u>blood</u>.
3) The <u>skeleton</u> is described as "the chassis or cage or cathedral of bone" — this gives an idea of it being a big <u>structure</u>, like a car or a building.
4) In lines 9-12, the poet describes his body as if it's a <u>shop</u>, an <u>engine</u>, <u>clothes</u> and a <u>clock</u>.

Before You Were Mine (Pages 44-45)

Before

1) The poet uses imagery to describe the life her <u>mother</u> had, before she was born.
2) The <u>images</u> are quite <u>nostalgic</u> — they describe <u>memories</u> of her mum playing on a street corner, staying out late and dancing. These are things she wouldn't do in the same way again, once she settled down and had kids.
3) She uses <u>glamorous language</u> to describe her mother's younger self: "Marilyn", "fizzy, movie tomorrows", "high-heeled red shoes", "scent", "sparkle". This creates an image of a <u>fun-loving, young girl</u>, full of <u>hopes</u> and <u>dreams</u>.

After

Some Poets use Imagery to Describe Places

Patrolling Barnegat (Pages 18-19)

1) The poet describes watchmen patrolling the beach during a <u>fierce storm</u>. He uses imagery to create a sense of how strong and frightening the storm is.
2) He describes the bad weather as if it is a <u>violent, attacking force</u> — e.g. "savagest trinity lashing".
3) The <u>sound of the gale</u> is described as if it's a <u>person's voice</u>: there's an "incessant undertone muttering" and sometimes it sounds like someone shrieking with "demoniac laughter".
4) He describes the <u>gloominess</u> of the scene with words like "midnight", "shadows" and "murk".

Inversnaid (Pages 32-33)

1) The poet describes a place he loves in the <u>countryside</u>. He makes an appeal for wild, natural places to be left as they are.
2) He builds up an image of the "<u>darksome burn</u>" in the first three verses. He emphasises the <u>colours</u>: the stream is "horseback brown", the lake "pitchblack" and the froth on the lake "fawn".
3) He also describes the <u>movement</u> of the place: the stream "roaring down" to the lake, the froth "turns and twindles" over the water, and the brook "treads through" the hills.

Imagery is an important poetic device...

Most poems have a bit of imagery in. It's a useful way for a poet to give a particular impression of something. Examples include: 'Anne Hathaway' (p.40-41), 'Mother, any distance' (p.52-53), 'Homecoming' (p.56-57), 'The Eagle' (p.24-25), 'Ulysses' (p.26-27) and 'Sonnet' (p.34-35).

Closing Couplets

A closing couplet is the <u>last 2 lines</u> of a poem.

---

1) A closing couplet can <u>sum up</u> the poem as a whole.

2) A closing couplet can make a <u>new</u> or <u>surprising point</u>, giving the poem an unexpected finish.

3) Closing couplets can be <u>set apart</u> from the rest of the poem, and sometimes they <u>rhyme</u>.

Closing Couplets can Sum Up a Poem

The Village Schoolmaster (Pages 28-29)

1) The closing couplet seems to <u>sum up</u> the poem, by telling us how the villagers were <u>baffled</u> by how much the schoolmaster knew.

2) There is some <u>uncertainty</u> too. The phrase "still the wonder grew" could mean that the villagers are impressed by the schoolmaster — but it might suggest that they <u>aren't sure</u> what to make of him.

"still the wonder grew"

I've made out a will (Pages 64-65)

1) The last two lines are <u>separate</u> from the rest of the poem. This <u>emphasises</u> the point they make.

2) The poem lists the parts of the poet's body that he's happy to <u>leave to the NHS</u>.

3) But the closing couplet says they <u>can't have his heart</u> — "not the pendulum, the ticker". The poet uses these two lines to make his wishes absolutely <u>clear</u>.

Closing Couplets can be Surprising

Sonnet 130 (Pages 20-21)

1) Shakespeare seems to be <u>criticising</u> his mistress, but the last two lines show he <u>does love her really</u>.

2) The closing couplet <u>surprises</u> the reader. It makes us look at the rest of the poem in a <u>different way</u>.

3) His love seems all the more <u>genuine</u> because he knows she's not perfect — "I think my love as rare / As any she belied with false compare."

November (Pages 58-59)

1) Most of this poem has a fairly <u>depressing</u> tone — the poet sees the old people in the home and they make him think about his own <u>death</u>.

2) In the closing couplet, the poet is a bit more <u>positive</u>. He says "the sun spangles" — he sees a <u>ray of light</u> and feels more <u>hopeful</u> when he thinks of the times that "we feel alive".

3) The poet concludes that people should <u>make the most</u> out of opportunities when they come up — "One thing we have to get, John, out of this life."

Closing couplets leave a lasting impression on the reader...

Other poems with interesting closing couplets are: 'Anne Hathaway' (p.40-41), 'On my first Sonne' (p.6-7), 'The Song of the Old Mother' (p.8-9) and 'Tichborne's Elegy' (p.14-15). Remember to write about how they relate to the rest of the poem.

Irony

Irony can be <u>funny</u>, but it can also be <u>tragic</u>.

1) It's ironic when <u>words</u> are used in a <u>sarcastic</u> or <u>comic</u> way to <u>imply the opposite</u> of what they normally mean. People often do this to draw attention to something being funny or odd.

2) It's ironic when there is a big <u>difference</u> between what people <u>expect or hope for</u> and <u>what actually happens</u>.

Sometimes the Whole Poem is Ironic

Tichborne's Elegy (Pages 14-15)

1) The <u>irony</u> in this poem is that even though the poet is still <u>young</u> and <u>healthy</u>, his life is <u>almost over</u> because he is about to be executed: "My youth is spent, and yet I am not old".

2) Tichborne <u>repeats</u> this idea throughout the poem, with each line making clear the <u>bitter irony</u> of his situation: "And now I live, and now my life is done."

The Man He Killed (Pages 16-17)

1) The poet points out that the man he <u>shot dead</u> could have been his <u>friend</u> if they'd met in <u>different circumstances</u>.

2) It's ironic that, if they'd met "By some old ancient inn", rather than being lined up opposite each other across a battlefield, they would have been <u>having a drink</u> together instead of <u>shooting</u> at each other.

Kid (Pages 60-61)

1) Robin <u>sarcastically</u> calls Batman a "big shot" — people used to think Batman was a big <u>hero</u>.

2) Now things have <u>changed</u>. Robin's the "real boy wonder" and Batman's <u>lonely</u> and <u>poor</u> — Robin pictures Batman "stewing over / chicken giblets in the pressure cooker".

3) It seems <u>ironic</u> that things have turned out this way, and Robin takes <u>pleasure</u> in pointing out this irony: "Batman, it makes a <u>marvellous picture</u>".

Irony Can Come Out at the End of the Poem

Salome (Pages 42-43)

1) This poem has lots of words which seem to have perfectly <u>innocent</u> meanings at first, but seem a lot more <u>suspicious</u> when we find out what has actually happened at the end of the poem.

2) The man's "rather matted" hair and "crimson mouth" turn out to be like that because the woman has <u>killed</u> him — they're covered in <u>blood</u>.

3) The phrase "ain't life a bitch" is said <u>ironically</u> — the character doesn't really care about the dead man.

Those bastards in their mansions (Pages 62-63)

1) The character in the poem says he's <u>innocent</u> of all the things he's been <u>accused</u> of — he hasn't "poisoned the dogs", "crossed the lawns" or "given heat and light to streets and houses".

2) Rather than starting a <u>revolution</u>, he says: "I stick to the shadows, carry a <u>gun</u>."

3) The <u>irony</u> is that he's actually planning something a lot more <u>serious</u> than the things he's denying. This irony only becomes clear in the <u>last line</u> of the poem.

Isn't it ironic...

Here are some other poems that have a spot of irony in them: 'Elvis's Twin Sister', (p.38-39), 'We Remember Your Childhood Well' (p.46-47), 'My father thought it bloody queer' (p.54-55), 'Hitcher' (p.66-67), 'My Last Duchess' (p.22-23) and 'The Laboratory' (p.30-31).

Language Effects

Language effects are the way the sounds of words in a poem are used to make a certain impression on the reader. Examples of language effects are alliteration, rhyme, assonance and onomatopoeia.

> 1) Language effects can create a mood or atmosphere in a poem.
> 2) Language effects can be useful for creating a vivid picture in the reader's mind of the place or person described in the poem.

Language Effects Can be Used to Describe Nature

Patrolling Barnegat (Pages 18-19)

1) There's half-rhyme throughout the poem, with each line ending in a verb with an "-ing" ending. These are mostly words to do with the movement of the wind and sea, e.g. "lashing", "careering", and this creates a fearsome, non-stop feel to the storm.
2) The poet uses onomatopoeia to create the effect of the sounds of the storm, e.g. the vowel sounds of "hoarse roar" remind us of the deep rumbling sounds of a fierce storm.
3) Alliteration of hard "c" sounds in "combs careering" makes the sea sound rough and dangerous.

Inversnaid (Pages 32-33)

1) Alliteration in the phrase "rollrock highroad roaring" makes the reader think of the roar of the water flowing down over the stony bed of the stream.
2) The harsh alliteration of "in coop and in comb" adds to the impression of a rugged setting.
3) In the last verse, the poet makes a point about how important it is to keep places like Inversnaid as they are. By repeating "w" sounds, the poet makes his point more effective, reminding us of the sounds of the countryside, like the wind blowing around the hills.

Language Effects Can be Used to Describe Feelings

Stealing (Pages 50-51)

1) The alliteration of "m" sounds in lines 2-4 creates an excited feel — the character is telling a story that he/she thinks is interesting.
2) The rhyming words in the poem show how the character sees certain things as being connected, e.g. "head" and "dead".
3) The rhyming is irregular, showing how the character's thoughts jump about fairly randomly — he/she seems rather unstable.

Kid (Pages 60-61)

1) Every line in the poem rhymes or half-rhymes, e.g. "order", "wander", "yonder", "rather". This gives the poem a relentless feel, reflecting Robin's accusing, sometimes mocking tone.
2) The repeated rhythm in "taller, harder, stronger, older" emphasises how much Robin has changed. This adds to the aggressive feel.
3) Alliteration in "next to nothing" and "punching the palm" make Robin's vision of Batman's downfall seem more dramatic and hard-hitting.

Language effects make descriptions more memorable...

Think about the effect each poet is trying to create. You could write about the language effects in these poems: 'The Eagle' (p.24-25), 'Sonnet' (p.34-35), 'Salome' (p.42-43) and 'Those bastards in their mansions' (p.62-63).

Mood

Mood is the <u>feel</u> or <u>atmosphere</u> of a poem. There are loads of different kinds of mood, e.g. light-hearted, tense, comical, threatening.

> 1) Mood can be created by describing a particular <u>place</u>.
> 2) Poets can create a certain mood by describing <u>feelings</u> — their own or other people's.
> 3) The mood can <u>change</u> from one part of a poem to another.

Mood can Come from the Situation

Sonnet (Pages 34-35)

1) The poet creates a <u>peaceful</u>, <u>happy</u> mood. The poem starts with "I love", so it starts on a <u>positive</u> note.
2) There are lots of <u>pretty country images</u>, such as the "willow leaning half way o'er / The clear deep lake". These descriptions give the poem a <u>peaceful</u> feel.
3) There's plenty of <u>colour</u> too, which gives the feel of a bright, carefree summer's day.
4) The insects' "happy wings" and the description of the beetles playing make the scene seem <u>carefree</u> and <u>natural</u>.

Tichborne's Elegy (Pages 14-15)

1) The mood in this poem is <u>sad</u>, <u>regretful</u> and rather <u>bitter</u>.
2) Tichborne talks about how he's still <u>young</u> and fit, but his life will soon be <u>over</u> when he's <u>executed</u>. He seems <u>bitter</u> about his fate — "My feast of joy is but a dish of pain".
3) The poet constantly points out the <u>bitter irony</u> of his situation. The whole poem has a <u>miserable</u>, <u>desperate</u> tone.

Bitter, Chidiock?

Uncertainty can Create a Sinister Mood

We Remember Your Childhood Well (Pages 46-47)

1) This poem has an <u>unpleasant</u> mood. The person whose voice we hear keeps <u>denying</u> things, suggesting that something <u>very nasty</u> has gone on in the past.
2) We don't hear directly what's being denied, which adds to the <u>dark tone</u>. The phrase "Nobody hurt you" hints at <u>child abuse</u> of some kind.
3) The person talking tries to <u>confuse</u> the person who's made the accusations — "The moment's a blur".
4) The mood becomes even <u>darker</u> at the end of the poem. The "skidmarks of sin" suggest how <u>horrible</u> the past events must have been.

Homecoming (Pages 56-57)

1) The first line sets the tone for a <u>mysterious</u> poem: "Think, two things on their own and both at once".
2) There's a <u>tense</u> mood in this poem, as it's <u>difficult</u> to work out exactly what's going on and how the things described in the poem are <u>connected</u> to each other.
3) There's also <u>tension</u> between the person the poet is talking to and her mother — "You seeing red. Blue murder. Bed."
4) The "<u>silhouette</u>" of a man who "<u>wants to set things straight</u>" could seem <u>threatening</u>.

You'll probably never be in the mood for an exam...

Good poems to look at for this theme include: 'On my first Sonne' (p.6-7), 'The Affliction of Margaret' (p.10-11), 'Havisham' (p.36-37), 'Elvis's Twin Sister' (p.38-39) and 'Hitcher' (p.66-67).

Stage 1 — Planning

Before you write the essay, you've got to plan it. Spend ten minutes planning — that leaves you with fifty minutes for writing. Use this two-stage method to plan your essay:

A Read the Question Carefully and Underline Key Words

1) Read the question you've chosen a couple of times. The question will usually ask you how the poems show/present/use/convey the theme. Underline the theme and any other important words.

2) You have to compare four poems altogether. The question will give you the titles of some or all of the poems that you have to write about. If the question gives you a choice about which poems to write about, make sure you pick poems which relate to the theme the question is on.

3) Look up the poems you're going to write about in the copy of the Anthology you are given in the exam. Bend the corner over on those pages, so that you can find them again quickly.

EXAMPLE QUESTION

They want you to compare the poems.

The theme of this question is death.

Question 1	Compare how ideas about death are presented in four of the following poems.

Choose two poems from List A and two poems from List B.

List A
Salome (Duffy)
Education for Leisure (Duffy)
November (Armitage)

List B
The Man He Killed (Hardy)
On my first Sonne (Jonson)
The Laboratory (Browning)

Remember to compare the following in your answer:
• the feelings about death described in the poems
• the language used to describe death.

Refer to these two pointers throughout your answer.

B Spend 5-10 Minutes Planning your Essay

Write a plan at the top of your answer paper — this will help you write a good essay. Just scribble stuff down, like in the example below. At the end of the exam, draw a neat line through your plan, so the examiner knows that it's rough work.

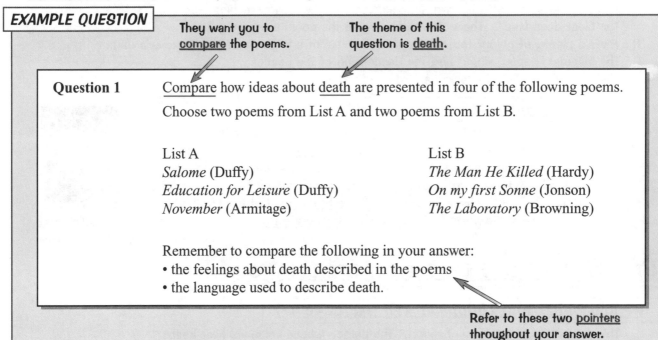

Plan - poems to write about: Education for Leisure, November, The Man He Killed, On my First Sonne

1) Intro about theme - death
2) Education
Excited by death
Wants to "play God"
3) November
Death is depressing/scary
Imagery - "terror of the dusk"

4) Man He Killed
Questions reasons for killing in war
Conversational language - sounds like he's thinking about it
5) First Sonne
Saddened by death but says maybe it's a good thing
Metaphorical lang - "fleshes rage"
6) Conc - preferred Man He Killed - seems most relevant today

Planning is the basis of a good essay...

Always write a plan. It'll help you get your ideas in order, and write a well-structured essay. Once you've got a plan, you know what you're going to write — it will give you confidence.

THIS IS A FLAP.
FOLD THIS PAGE OUT.

Sample Essay — Death

This is a sample answer to the exam question on page 84.

Intro. 1

Death is an emotional subject. For many poets, it is connected to feelings of grief, sadness and loss, for example, in Armitage's 'November' and Jonson's 'On my first Sonne'. Other poets show how death can seem strange, such as Hardy's 'The Man He Killed'. Duffy's poem, 'Education for Leisure', on the other hand, shows how death can seem thrilling to an unbalanced person.

Outline the ways the poems deal with the theme in the intro.

Poem 1 2

In 'Education for Leisure', the narrator sees death as something exciting that could be a way out of the boredom he/she is feeling. He/she wants "to play God", which suggests that causing death makes him/her feel important and powerful. Even though the killing begins with a fly, the narrator seems very proud of it, saying "I am a genius". The narrator has no sense that what he/she is doing is wrong. He/she is completely unaffected by normal attitudes to death, such as sadness and loss.

Try to work quotes into your sentences.

Poem 2 3

The narrator in 'November', on the other hand, is saddened and frightened by the idea of death. Seeing the old people in the nursing home shocks the narrator. Their "stunned brains" make them seem almost dead already. This makes the narrator think about his own death. The setting sun seems to be a metaphor for life coming to an end, and this scares the narrator: "we feel the terror of the dusk begin." However, like in 'Education for Leisure', the narrator takes something positive out of death, although in a very different way. Whereas in Duffy's poem, murder provides excitement, Armitage's narrator realises that the fact that we will all die means we should make the most out of life: "One thing we have to get, John, out of this life."

Keep discussing the theme — it's been highlighted in green in this essay.

Compare Poem 2 to Poem 1.

Poem 3 4

The feelings about death described in 'The Man He Killed' are calmer and more thoughtful than in the previous two poems. The narrator in Hardy's poem thinks about a soldier he killed in battle. He says that it is strange that he killed a man he might have been friends with if they had met "By some old ancient inn". He says that the man may well have been similar to him, joining the army because he "Was out of work — had sold his traps". The feelings about death in this poem seem less strong than those in Duffy's and Armitage's poems. The narrator appears to be confused rather than excited. He says that it is "quaint and curious" that war makes you kill people just because you happen to be on different sides.

Keep comparing the poems to the ones you've already discussed.

Poem 4 5

The feelings about death in 'On my first Sonne' at first seem more traditional than those in the other three poems. The poet is grief-stricken about the death of his son: "Farewell, thou child of my right hand, and joy". But Jonson then goes on to say that people should not "lament the state that they should envie", meaning death. The poet uses harsh language to describe getting old, such as having to put up with "worlds, and fleshes rage", suggesting that death is better than life. So Jonson's poem, like that of Armitage, shows that death can be a good thing. The difference is that Jonson sees life as painful, whereas Armitage sees death as a good reason to make the most of life.

Write about similarities and differences between the poems.

Conclusion 6

These four poems all explore feelings about death. 'November' and 'On my first Sonne' both show how death can be devastating, but may also have a positive side. The character in 'Education for Leisure' also sees death as a good thing, but for more immoral and evil reasons. My favourite of these four poems is 'The Man He Killed', as Hardy's point about the deaths caused by war seems particularly appropriate at the moment, when so many people are still being killed in wars every day.

Say what your feelings about the poems are in the conclusion.

Stage 2 — Writing

FOLLOW THIS SIX-STEP METHOD FOR A GOOD ANSWER EVERY TIME

Don't forget — each of these steps needs a paragraph of its own.

① Write about the Theme in the Introduction

1) Give a <u>definition</u>. It doesn't have to be detailed — just describe what you think the theme means.

2) Briefly <u>explain</u> how the theme is explored in each of the poems you're going to write about.

② Write about the First Poem

1) Write about how the first poem relates to the <u>theme</u> of the question. A couple of sentences will do.

2) Remember to use the <u>pointers</u> — they're there to make your life easier.

> You can adapt this method for doing 2-part questions. There's an example on pages 86-87.

③ Write about the Second Poem

1) Write about how the second poem relates to the <u>theme</u> of the question in another couple of sentences.

2) Use the <u>pointers</u> and stick to the <u>theme</u> — don't go rambling off about something irrelevant.

3) <u>Compare</u> the second poem to the first — say if they're similar or different, or a bit of both. Here are a few words and phrases you can use to show that you're comparing the poems:

• in contrast	• although	• more	• conversely
• on the other hand	• however	• less	• but
• similarly	• unlike	• in the same way	• also

④ Write about the Third Poem

1) Write about how the third poem relates to the <u>theme</u> of the question.

2) Keep referring to the <u>pointers</u>.

3) <u>Compare</u> the third poem to the first and second poems (<u>unless</u> it's a two part question).

⑤ Write about the Fourth Poem

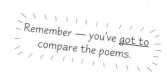

> Remember — you've <u>got to</u> compare the poems.

1) Write about how the fourth poem relates to the <u>theme</u> of the question.

2) Keep referring to the <u>pointers</u>.

3) <u>Compare</u> the fourth poem to the first, second and third poems — <u>unless</u> it's a two part question, in which case, just compare the fourth poem to the third.

4) Don't worry about this poem as much as the others if you're really pressed for time. Make one good point, compare the poems, and then move on to a really good conclusion.

⑥ Give a Personal Response to the Poems in the Conclusion

1) Briefly <u>compare</u> the poems again.

2) Say which poem you <u>preferred</u> and why — examiners love it when you do this.

And finally — don't forget to check through your work...

We've included some '<u>C</u>' grade essay answers on the next few pages. They use the method described here and should give you a good idea of what you're aiming for...

Sample Essay — Characters

Here's an example of a two-part question — and how to answer it well...

A Here's an Exam-style Question about Characters

Question 1   You should answer both parts (a) and (b).

(a)   Compare how poets portray characters in *Kid* by Simon Armitage and *The Laboratory* by Robert Browning.

(b)   Compare the ways characters are presented in *Havisham* by Carol Ann Duffy and one more poem from the Pre-1914 Poetry Bank.

Remember to compare the following in both parts of your answer:
- the personalities of the characters in the poems
- how the poets present the characters.

B Here's an Example of a Plan for this Answer

Plan: poems to write about: Kid, The Laboratory, Havisham, The Village Schoolmaster

PART (A)	PART (B)
1) Intro about theme - characters	Intro to part (b)
2) Kid	4) Havisham
Narrator is bitter, wants revenge	V. angry but confused emotions
Narr. shows Batman is irresponsible/immoral	Described as if she's an animal
3) Lab	5) Schoolmaster
Obsessed with revenge	Frightening but skilful.
We hear her voice directly	Villagers find him mysterious
Conclusion for part (a)	6) Conclusion for part (b)
Characters in 'Kid' more realistic	'Havisham' character more interesting

Here's a 'C' Grade Answer to the Question

Introduction

1

(a) Characters are the people whose personalities, emotions or actions are portrayed in a poem. In 'Kid', Simon Armitage describes the character of a young adult getting revenge on the person who failed to look after him properly when he was growing up. Similarly, the main character in Robert Browning's poem, 'The Laboratory', is also looking for revenge, by preparing to poison the mistress of her husband or lover.

Briefly discuss the theme in the introduction.

Poem 1

2

There are two characters in 'Kid': the narrator and "Batman", his guardian. The narrator is very bitter about the way Batman treated him, saying that he "gave the order / to grow up". The narrator wants to prove that he has come through his difficult experiences. He tells Batman, "now I'm taller, harder, older, stronger". The idea of the narrator's energy and strength is added to by the fast rhythm of this line. Batman is portrayed as immoral, and the narrator shows that he was not the "father figure" that other people thought he was. We are told how Batman took a married woman "downtown on expenses in the motor", and the word "caper" makes him seem like a villain rather than a hero.

The key words from the question are highlighted in green.

Treat each part of the question, (a) and (b), like a mini-essay.

Sample Essay — Characters

Poem 2 **3**

In 'The Laboratory', the poet presents the main character as obsessed with getting revenge on her husband or lover by poisoning his mistress. The narrator in this poem is more scheming than Batman in 'Kid'. She plans to murder her rival and does not seem to care about right or wrong. She says, "He is sure to remember her dying face!", suggesting she takes pleasure from the horrific details of the murder. One similarity she has with the narrator in 'Kid' is her single-mindedness. She describes the poisons as "treasures", suggesting they are more valuable to her than anything else.

Compare Poem 2 with Poem 1.

Back up your points with quotes from the poem.

Conclusion

Both of these poems give a clear impression of the characters in them. The narrator in 'Kid' is similar to the woman in 'The Laboratory' in that they are both determined to gain revenge. I prefer the depiction of the characters in 'Kid', as they seem similar to real-life people, whereas the dramatically evil woman in 'The Laboratory' seems less realistic.

Include a conclusion for part (a).

Introduction

(b) Poets can present characters in straightforward or more complicated ways. In 'Havisham', the poet describes an unstable character who is still extremely bitter about being rejected on her wedding day years earlier. The character described in 'The Village Schoolmaster', on the other hand, is less clear-cut, as the poet gives a confusing impression of him.

The question's in two parts, so answer each part separately.

Poem 3 **4**

In 'Havisham', Carol Ann Duffy portrays the narrator as a very violent but also confused character. The first sentence, "Beloved sweetheart bastard", shows her complicated feelings towards the man who rejected her. She is full of hatred for him, yet she also desperately wants him to come back. Duffy presents Havisham as having become like an animal because of what has happened to her. For example, the word "cawing" creates an image of her screeching like a crow. The imagery of "Love's / hate behind a white veil" adds to the impression of this character being torn between strong, conflicting emotions.

Remember to use the pointers in the question.

Poem 4 **5**

In contrast, the character described in Oliver Goldsmith's poem, 'The Village Schoolmaster', seems more mysterious. The language the poet uses to describe the schoolmaster give us an uncertain idea of what he was like. On the one hand, he was "A man severe", who children were so frightened of they pretended to laugh at his jokes. But the narrator also tells us, "he was kind", and there is a tone of admiration as we are told of all his knowledge and skills. The phrase that seems to sum up the schoolmaster is "still the wonder grew". We do not know what to make of him, as, unlike Havisham whose strong feelings are clear, the description of the schoolmaster is vague and contradictory.

Try to write roughly the same amount for parts (a) and (b).

Conc. **6**

Two very different characters are described in 'Havisham' and 'The Village Schoolmaster'. Duffy's poem is about a person who has lost control, whereas Goldsmith portrays an odd, mysterious character. I find Havisham a more interesting character, as I find her mix of hatred and longing gripping and fascinating.

Give a personal response in the conclusion.

Sample Essay — Imagery

Some of the exam questions will be about <u>poetic methods</u> e.g. imagery, use of first person, closing couplets. Don't be scared off by these questions — you can still answer them using the 6-step method (see p.85). Here's an example.

Here's an Exam-style Question about Imagery

| Question 1 | Compare the ways poets use imagery in four poems from this selection. Compare *My father thought it bloody queer* by Simon Armitage, one poem by Carol Ann Duffy and two poems from the Pre-1914 Poetry Bank.

Remember to compare the following in your answer:
• the effect of the imagery used in the poems
• how the poets use imagery to show feelings. |

Here's an Example of a Plan for this Answer

Plan – poems to write about: My father thought it bloody queer, Before You Were Mine, Sonnet, The Eagle

1) Intro about theme - imagery
2) My father
Imagery shows pain at memory
Shows narrator's emotions at becoming like dad
3) Before
Imagery creates glamorous feel
Mother was young/vibrant

4) Sonnet
Colours make images vivid
Peaceful imagery echoes poet's happiness
5) Eagle
Imagery shows strength/height of eagle
Shows poet's admiration for eagle
6) Conclusion - preferred sonnet

Here's a 'C' Grade Answer to the Question

Intro.

1

Imagery is the way poets use language to create vivid descriptions of situations, events and even emotions. In Simon Armitage's poem, 'My father thought it bloody queer' and Carol Ann Duffy's 'Before You Were Mine', imagery is used to describe memories. In other poems such as 'Sonnet' by John Clare and Alfred Tennyson's 'The Eagle', imagery is used to portray nature.

Briefly introduce the theme and how it relates to the poems in your answer.

Poem 1

2

In 'My father thought it bloody queer', the narrator describes a time when, as a teenager, he had his ear pierced and his father mocked him. It is a painful memory. He says that the piercing "became a wound, and wept", and this imagery suggests both the physical pain of the piercing and his hurt feelings at his father's reaction. The imagery in the final stanza describes the narrator's pain at realising that he now says the same things to young people that his father used to say to him. He describes "my own voice breaking like a tear", suggesting the thought of it almost makes him cry.

You have to back up your points with good quotes from the poems.

Sample Essay — Imagery

Poem 2

3

Similarly, Duffy uses imagery to describe emotions that are linked to memories. Unlike those in Armitage's poem, the memories in 'Before You Were Mine' are described mostly with fondness rather than pain. Duffy uses imagery to create a glamorous, carefree picture of what her mother was like before the poet was born. She describes "the fizzy, movie tomorrows", and this makes her mother's past sound exciting. She says "now your ghost clatters toward me", which shows that her mother's fun-loving lifestyle is a thing of the past. The poet sums up the carefree impression of her mother as "the bold girl winking in Portobello", an image which makes her seem happy and confident.

Show how the poems are similar or different by using words like "similarly" or "in contrast".

Explain the effect of the quotes you use.

Poem 3

4

The imagery in 'Sonnet', however, is used to describe a scene in the present, rather than in the past as in Armitage and Duffy's poems. The imagery is also used to describe simpler and clearer feelings. He says "I love to see the wild flowers come again", which is a typical image of early summer. A lot of the imagery in this poem uses colours, such as "water lilies whiten". This gives a bright, natural feel to the poem, emphasising why the poet loves the summer so much. Clare also describes a lot of gentle movement, such as "the flower head swings", which further adds to the peaceful feel of the scene, reflecting the poet's happiness.

The key words in the question are highlighted in green.

Poem 4

5

Like 'Sonnet', 'The Eagle' contains a lot of natural imagery, and the poet, Tennyson, also uses it to show positive feelings about nature. However, while Clare describes how happy a peaceful summer scene makes him feel, Tennyson shows his admiration for the ruggedness of an eagle. He describes the eagle as "Close to the sun", which shows that the eagle is very high up as he stands on the cliff. The phrase "mountain walls" creates the impression that the eagle is the owner of a massive house made out of the cliffs. When the eagle swoops down to catch his prey, the poet describes him as "like a thunderbolt", bringing home the amazing speed of the eagle, and all these pieces of imagery create an impressive, powerful image.

Keep the theme in mind throughout your answer.

Be careful to leave time to write about all four poems.

Conclusion

6

Imagery is important to the effect of all four of these poems. In "My father thought it bloody queer" and "Before You Were Mine", Armitage and Duffy use it to express the different feelings they have about things that happened in the past, whereas, in 'Sonnet' and 'The Eagle', Clare and Tennyson describe positive, natural images. I particularly like the imagery in 'The Eagle' as I find its speed and strength striking and impressive.

Keep comparing the poems all the way through.

Always put in a conclusion.

Sample Essay — Attitudes Towards Other People

Read through this sample essay for some <u>handy tips</u> on how to write a fantastic essay.
<u>Key words</u> have been highlighted in green — both in the question and the answer.

Here's an Exam-style Question about Attitudes to Other People

Question 1   Compare how attitudes towards other people are presented in *On my first Sonne* by Ben Jonson, *The Song of the Old Mother* by William Butler Yeats, one poem by Simon Armitage and one poem by Carol Ann Duffy.

Remember to compare the following in both parts of your answer:
- the feelings expressed in the poems
- the way the poets express these feelings.

Here's an Example of a Plan for this Answer

<u>Plan</u> – On my First Sonne, The Song of the Old Mother, Anne Hathaway, Those bastards in their mansions

1) Intro – attitudes to other people	4) Anne
2) First Sonne	Loving, fond memories of Shakespeare
Proud of his son	Says he lives on in her mind
Fond memories	5) Bastards
3) Old Mother	Narrator hates rich people
Says young people are lazy	Sees them in stereotyped way
Only interested in silly things	6) Conclusion – preferred Anne

Here's a 'C' Grade Answer to the Question

Introduction
1

    The attitudes that poets express about other people can be positive or negative. In 'On my first Sonne', the poet says a fond goodbye to his son, who has died aged just seven, while the narrator of 'The Song of the Old Mother' criticises young people for being lazy. 'Anne Hathaway' is about a widow's loving memories of her dead husband, while the character in 'Those bastards in their mansions' has violent, resentful feelings towards rich people.

Start by talking about the theme.

Poem 1
2

    In 'On my first Sonne', Ben Jonson describes his feelings about his dead son. The poet was clearly very fond of his son, describing him as "thou child of my right hand" and "lov'd boy". He is so proud of him that he describes him as his "best piece of poetrie", suggesting that he considers his son to be a greater creation than any of his famous poems. The poet is grateful for the time he had with his son. He manages to take something positive from his death, by saying that he has "scap'd worlds, and fleshes rage".

Always keep the theme of the question in mind.

Remember to use quotes to back up your points.

Sample Essay — Attitudes Towards Other People

Poem 2

3

Jonson's love for his son contrasts with the narrator's feelings about young people in 'The Song of the Old Mother'. The old woman describes how she works all day long without rest, and contrasts this with how "the young lie long and dream in their beds". This shows us how unfair the situation is. The narrator goes on to say that "their day goes over in idleness", and here she seems to resent their laziness. The woman also says that young people are very quick to complain about the smallest amount of inconvenience or discomfort: "they sigh if the wind but lift a tress". Again, this contrasts with the old woman, who must put up quietly with the aches and pains of her constant work.

Try to write roughly the same amount about each of the poems if possible.

Poem 3

4

The attitudes described in 'Anne Hathaway', like those in 'On my first Sonne' are positive and loving. Both poems are about feelings for a dead loved one, in the case of 'Anne Hathaway', her husband. Anne fondly recalls the magical time she spent with Shakespeare. She compares their love with the way he wrote his plays: "his touch / a verb dancing in the centre of a noun". Similarly, Jonson compares his son to a poem, calling him his "best piece of poetrie". Anne's memories of Shakespeare him seem to excite her. She describes his words as "shooting stars which fell to earth as kisses / on these lips", suggesting that the time they had together was very romantic.

Don't just stick quotes in — show that you know what they mean and what effect they create.

Poem 4

5

In stark contrast to 'Anne Hathaway' and 'On my first Sonne', the attitudes towards other people that are described in 'Those bastards in their mansions' are hateful and aggressive. The narrator has a stereotyped view of rich people, describing them as "Those lords and ladies in their palaces and castles". The narrator also presents rich people as weak and nervous, saying that they "shriek" as if he was breaking into their houses. He also describes them as bullies, saying that they would have him "picked at by their eagles".

Say which poems are similar and which are different.

Conclusion

6

The attitudes towards other people in these poems vary between positive memories of loved ones, as in 'On my first Sonne' and 'Anne Hathaway', and the negative, critical descriptions in 'The Song of the Old Mother' and 'Those bastards in their mansions'. I find 'Anne Hathaway' the most interesting of these four poems. Anne sums up her feelings for her husband by describing him as "My living laughing love", which I think is a beautiful and touching way of remembering him.

Start the conclusion by drawing together your main points.

Include a personal response to make the conclusion interesting.

Glossary

adjective	A word that <u>describes</u> something, e.g. "big", "fast", "annoying".
alliteration	Where words <u>start</u> with the <u>same letter</u>. It's often used in poetry to give a nice pattern to a phrase. E.g. '<u>S</u>ally's <u>s</u>lipper <u>s</u>lipped on a <u>s</u>limy <u>s</u>lug.'
ambiguity	Where a word or phrase has <u>two or more</u> possible <u>meanings</u>.
assonance	When words share the same vowel sound but the consonants are different. E.g. "L<u>i</u>sa had a p<u>ie</u>ce of ch<u>ee</u>se before sh<u>e</u> went to sl<u>ee</u>p, to help her dr<u>ea</u>m."
blank verse	Poetry that <u>doesn't rhyme</u>, usually in <u>iambic pentameters</u>.
colloquial	Sounding like everyday <u>spoken</u> language.
compound word	A word that is made up of two or more other words <u>put together</u>, e.g. "flame-red".
consonants	All the letters in the alphabet that <u>aren't vowels</u>.
contrast	When two things are described in a way which emphasises <u>how different</u> they are. E.g. a poet might contrast two different places or two different people.
dialect	<u>Regional variation</u> of a <u>language</u>. People from different places might use different words or sentence constructions. E.g. In some northern English dialects, people might say "Ey up" instead of "Hello".
empathy	When someone feels like they <u>understand</u> what someone else is experiencing and how they <u>feel</u> about it.
enjambement	When a sentence runs over from <u>one line</u> to the <u>next</u>.
iambic pentameter	This is a form of poetry that doesn't rhyme, but usually has a clear <u>metre</u> of <u>ten syllables</u> — five of them stressed, and five unstressed. The <u>stress</u> falls on <u>every second syllable</u>, e.g. "Co<u>ral</u> is <u>far</u> more <u>red</u> than <u>her</u> lips' <u>red</u>."
imagery	Language that creates a <u>picture in your mind</u>.
irony	When <u>words</u> are used in a <u>sarcastic</u> or <u>comic</u> way to <u>imply the opposite</u> of what they normally mean. It can also mean when there is a big difference between <u>what people expect</u> and <u>what actually happens</u>.
language	The <u>choice of words</u> used. The language determines the effect the piece of writing will have on the reader, e.g. it can be emotive or persuasive.
layout	The way a piece of poetry is visually <u>presented</u> to the reader. E.g. line length, whether the poem is broken up into different stanzas, whether lines are arranged regularly or create some kind of visual pattern.
metaphor	A way of describing something by saying that it <u>is something else</u>, to create a vivid image. E.g. "His eyes were deep, black, oily pools."
metre	The arrangement of syllables to create <u>rhythm</u> in a line of poetry.
mood	The <u>feel</u> or <u>atmosphere</u> of a poem, e.g. humorous, threatening, eerie.
mythology	A collection of very old <u>stories</u>, often involving gods and heroes. Different cultures have their own mythologies.
narrator	The <u>voice</u> speaking the words that you're reading. E.g. a poem could be written from the point of view of a young child, which means the young child is the poem's narrator.

Glossary

noun	A word for a <u>place</u>, <u>person</u> or <u>thing</u>, e.g. "tree", "air", "Boris", "London".
onomatopoeia	A word that <u>sounds like</u> the thing it's describing. E.g. "buzz", "crunch", "bang", "pop", "ding".
persona	A <u>fictional character</u> or <u>identity</u> adopted by a poet. Poets often create a persona so they can describe things from a different person's <u>point of view</u>, e.g. a male poet might use a female persona.
personification	A special kind of metaphor where you write about something as if it's a <u>person</u> with thoughts and feelings. E.g. "The sea growled hungrily."
phonetic spelling	When words are <u>spelt</u> as they <u>sound</u> rather than with their usual spelling. It's often used to show that someone's speaking with a certain <u>accent</u>.
rhyme scheme	A regular <u>system</u> of rhyming words in a poem, e.g. in 'The Man He Killed', the 1st line of each verse rhymes with the 3rd, and the 2nd rhymes with the 4th.
rhyming couplet	A pair of lines that are next to each other and whose final words <u>rhyme</u>.
rhythm	When sentences or lines have a <u>regular fixed pattern</u> of syllables.
simile	A way of describing something by <u>comparing</u> it to something else, usually by using the words "like" or "as". E.g. "He was as pale as the moon," or "Her hair was like a bird's nest."
sonnet	A type of poem with <u>fourteen lines</u>, and usually following a <u>clear rhyme pattern</u>. There are different popular patterns for sonnets. They will often have ten syllables a line, and end with a rhyming couplet.
stanza	A <u>group of lines</u> in a poem that often share the same rhythm pattern and have similar line lengths. Stanzas can also be called <u>verses</u>.
stereotype	An inaccurate, <u>generalised</u> view of a particular <u>group of people</u>. E.g. A stereotype of football fans might be that they're all hooligans.
structure	The <u>order</u> and arrangement of a piece of writing. E.g. how the poem begins, develops and ends, whether it uses verses or not, whether it has a particular layout, etc.
syllable	A single <u>unit of sound</u> within a word. E.g. "all" has one syllable, "always" has two and "establishmentarianism" has nine.
symbolism	When an object <u>stands for something else</u>. E.g. a candle might be a symbol of hope, or a dying flower could symbolise the end of a relationship.
syntax	The way a sentence is put together so that it <u>makes sense</u>.
theme	An <u>idea</u> or <u>topic</u> that's important in a piece of writing. E.g. a poem could be based on the theme of friendship.
verb	A word that describes something you <u>do</u>, e.g. "run", "talk", "hope".
vocabulary	All the <u>words</u> used in a piece of writing.
voice	The <u>personality</u> narrating the poem. Poems are usually written either using the poet's voice, as if they're speaking to you <u>directly</u>, or the voice of a <u>character</u>, e.g. an elderly man, or a horse.
vowels	Simple — the letters 'a', 'e', 'i', 'o' and 'u'.

Index

Index

The Publisher would like to thank:

Poets:

Carol Ann Duffy 'Elvis's Twin Sister', 'Anne Hathaway' and 'Salome' from *The World's Wife* (Picador Macmillan, 1999),
© Carol Ann Duffy 1999, reprinted by permission of the publisher, Macmillan, London, UK.
'Education for Leisure' is taken from *Standing Female Nude* by Carol Ann Duffy published by Anvil Press Poetry in 1985.
'Stealing' is taken from *Selling Manhattan* by Carol Ann Duffy published by Anvil Press Poetry in 1987.
'Havisham' and 'Before You Were Mine' are taken from *Mean Time* by Carol Ann Duffy published by Anvil Press Poetry in 1993.
'We Remember Your Childhood Well' is taken from *The Other Country* by Carol Ann Duffy published by Anvil Press Poetry in 1990.

Simon Armitage 'Hitcher', 'Those bastards in their mansions', 'My father thought it bloody queer', 'Mother', 'Kid', 'I've made out
a will' and 'Homecoming' from *Selected Poems* (2001) all reprinted by permission of the publishers, Faber & Faber Ltd.
'November' Simon Armitage, *ZOOM!* (Bloodaxe Books, 1989).

William Butler Yeats 'The Song of the Old Mother' published by permission of A.P. Watt Ltd. on behalf of Michael B. Yeats

Image sources:

Image of Carol Ann Duffy © Anvil Press

Images of Ben Jonson, William Wordsworth, William Blake, John Clare, Thomas Hardy, Walt Whitman,
Robert Browning, Alfred Lord Tennyson and Oliver Goldsmith © Mary Evans Picture Library

Images of William Butler Yeats and Gerard Manley Hopkins © National Portrait Gallery, London

Image of William Shakespeare © Royal Shakespeare Company

Image of Simon Armitage © www.roderickfield.com

*Every effort has been made to locate copyright holders and obtain permission to reproduce poems and images. For those
poems and images where it has been difficult to trace the originator of the work, we would be grateful for information. If any
copyright holder would like us to make an amendment to the acknowledgements, please notify us and we will gladly update the
book at the next reprint. Thank you.*